COUNTRY HAM

A SOUTHERN TRADITION OF
HOGS, SALT & SMOKE

STEVE COOMES

AMERICAN PALATE

Published by American Palate

A Division of The History Press

Charleston, SC 29403

www.historypress.net

Copyright © 2014 by Steve Coomes

All rights reserved

Cover images: Front cover photo by author. Back top image courtesy of S. Wallace Edwards & Sons.

All photos by author unless otherwise noted.

First published 2014

Manufactured in the United States

ISBN 978.1.62619.330.7

Library of Congress CIP data applied for.

CONTENTS

ACKNOWLEDGEMENTS

I've heard would-be or actual authors say often, "I've got a book in me. I just need to get it out." I've honestly never felt that way—never had "a book in me" or a desire just to "get it out." As a journalist, my job is to tell other people's stories, to chronicle their lives for others to enjoy. Their stories don't add up to "a book in me" because all I'm doing is sharing the details of events experienced by someone else. I merely transfer the highlights to paper or the Internet or weave them into conversation.

Early on in the creation of this book, I decided that the stories of the people profiled were best left told by them, not reshaped by my limited skills or the indelicate tools of the trade. Any child of the South knows that books don't live up to the storytelling skills of a southerner. Even the best authors can't match a live storyteller's emotions, voice inflections, expressions and cadence. To preserve as much of that as I could, I've done my best to get out of the way and let them do the talking. I can't thank these people enough for taking the time to share their stories with me. Without them, there is no book.

I also must acknowledge so many others who've been instrumental in this effort:

To my wife, Leslie, and son, Kyle, for putting up with my irritability and extended absences for nearly a year. I'm so looking forward to more date nights and evenings fishing together.

To my brother, Mark, whose thoughtful and skillful editing of this book taught me so much and made mop-up duty an easy chore for the team at

The History Press. Thanks for your patient guidance and mentorship. Oh, and yours is next, so get on it.

To my mother, Mary Ann Thompson, who taught me that hard work is a good thing. This was hard, Mom, but it was good for me.

To my seventh-grade language arts teacher, Rosemary Newton, who praised an assignment of mine by reading it out loud to the class. That thirty-second compliment went a long way in a struggling student's life. It has stuck with me for thirty-seven years.

To my English 102 professor (whose name I can't recall) at the University of Louisville, who told me, "You're a decent writer, but I don't think you can make a living at it." It bothered me some when you said it, but maybe I was just too stupid to believe you were right. I can't tell you how much fun it's been proving you wrong for the past twenty-three years.

To Richard Lewis, who kept me laughing throughout the assembly of this work and cheered me on when it got tiring. I can't wait to see how our country hams turn out this fall.

To the many chefs and home cooks who shared their recipes.

To Nancy Newsom, for sending me that sample box of your exquisite country ham in 2009. Had your see-through, prosciutto-style slivers not triggered my personal pork epiphany, this book might never have been written.

And to Jesus Christ, my lord and savior. Please help me do a better job of telling your story.

IT'S ALL NANCY'S FAULT

On a late January morning in 2013, the temperature inside my friend's garage in Brooks, Kentucky, is eighteen degrees. Richard Lewis and I are rubbing a salt-and-sugar cure into the cracks, crevices and flesh folds of eight fresh hams. Our plastic gloves provide no protection from the finger-numbing chill, but I'm not complaining. Professionals do this for hours at a time, hand-curing thousands of hams during a single shift, the first step in transforming those hindquarters into savory salt-cured meat.

A few weeks before Richard and I got our introduction to curing, I'd traveled to Clifty Farm Country Meats in Paris, Tennessee, where employees cure 750,000 hams per year. The company uses plenty of machinery, but the basics of turning an ordinary ham into a Clifty creation differs little from this morning's old-fashioned work. Whether the operation is massive or small, the curers pros or rank amateurs, making country hams requires just three essentials: hogs, salt and smoke. Well, and time. Lots of time. Aged a minimum of six months—more commonly nine and increasingly twelve to twenty-four months—country ham arguably is the least hurried of all slow foods. By comparison, fermenting kimchi takes five days, sauerkraut one month and Chinese thousand-year eggs stay buried ninety days. Such waits seem like a trip to the vending machine compared to ham aging.

So, as we rub cure into our hams, it's a little disheartening to think that we'll have to wait until the fall to learn if they're any good, to see if I listened closely enough during the dozens of discussions I had with curers about this centuries-old craft. When we taste our hams in October, we'll know instantly whether we're proud enough to share them with others. About six hours after that, our stomachs will let us know if we conquered bacteria in the "battle to the bone." The odds are super long that our meat will wind up tainted with trichinosis, but if we lose, it won't be pretty. (Thankfully there are several pre-consumption safeguards for that.)

If the cure works and our hams are good, maybe the best part will be calling Nancy Newsom to celebrate. Newsom—owner and curer at Col. Bill Newsom's Aged Kentucky Country Ham in Princeton, Kentucky—is a big reason why we're here this morning, wrist deep in cure, working in this frigid, thin-skinned garage, when we should be busy with our day jobs, when we could be eating someone else's proven product or when we could read about others who've done it. But where's the fun in that? We're trying it out for ourselves.

Here's why Newsom matters to this pork project. In 2009, I wrote an article about her traveling to Huelva, Spain, as a guest of that nation's *V Congreso Mundial del Jamón* (Fifth World Congress of Ham). The country lady was a doubly novel attraction: the first American artisan invited to bring ham to the Congress, and a woman in a profession nearly exclusive to men. Newsom's homespun personality so charmed the Spaniards that, despite her unfamiliarity with their language, she was interviewed on national television. The *Congreso* even honored her by requesting that she leave one of her hams for display in their ham museum.

After the story ran, a UPS package from Newsom arrived at my door. The smiling driver knew well of its contents and promised, "Oh, you're going to like this. This is really good ham."

Over my career writing about food, I'd gotten unsolicited samples of beef, spices, tequila, beer, bourbon, cheeses and candy, but salty ham swag was a first. Inside was a thank-you note from Nancy and multiple vacuum-sealed slices of her aged ham. Jackpot!

Dinner was only two hours away, but I deemed it snack time and cut open a package of paper-thin slices from a two-year-old ham. The flavor was complex yet mild, plenty piggy and earthy. It tasted like the animal it came from, not overprocessed and gummy like some country hams. It wasn't the super-salty, shoe-leathery stuff I'd eaten as a kid. It was so tender it barely required chewing. Recalling it makes my mouth water.

You'd think that growing up in Kentucky, the heart of "America's Country Ham Belt" (an oblong collection of states including Virginia, North Carolina, Tennessee, Kentucky and Missouri), would have long ago acquainted me with good country ham, but the opposite is mostly true. Not because of any lack of the good stuff, but because of how poorly it's commonly prepared: ruined from overcooking and never served like charcuterie.

Newsom's ham reminded me of the prosciutto I'd eaten at an Italian restaurant where I worked as a teenager—draped over cantaloupe or honeydew melon, slivered atop creamy pasta dishes or simply sliced for antipasto. I thought it delicious back then, but Newsom's was far better. It blew away the sinewy factory-made prosciutto that restaurant served.

Newsom's country ham was so good that I broke a personal cardinal rule about working from home: no alcohol before 5:00 p.m. Any wine, much less wine drunk at home in silence, makes me want to nap. But water wasn't good enough for Nancy's ham. It deserved something special to elevate its flavors, a liquid to honor that incredible pork. I uncorked a pricey Rioja, a special-occasion bottle stashed in a dark cabinet, and poured a glass. If I saved my wife some of both, I knew she wouldn't begrudge me the indulgence. (I was right. She got her share for dinner.)

As I chewed and sipped, the ham's flavors became even more familiar, like the *jamón Ibérico* slices I'd tasted two years before at a large gathering of chefs and food producers in Napa Valley, California. A man there carved see-through slices of Spain's preeminent ham, which when exported whole to the United States costs as much as $1,500 each.

The meat was magnificent, and his story was compelling. The hogs are pasture-raised and allowed plenty of room to graze. No factory pens or concrete floors are used there. During their final months alive, they eat acorns from oak forest bottoms, which impart flavorful, fatty nutrients to their systems. Exercise drives that dietary fat deep into their muscles, producing unrivaled marbling. The meat's luscious and long streaks of fat sweated and glistened at room temperature as he spoke. With only a tinge of shame, I returned to his booth too often.

Yet while Newsom's product was different, it was no less flavorful and cost just a tenth as much as the fabled *Ibérico*. Plus, hers was a Kentucky-made product, and I'd later learn that most of her hams come from commodity hogs, not pampered free-range pork.

Two years later, a restaurant named Garage Bar opened in downtown Louisville and served a country ham platter that remains one of its most popular items. Mind you, this "platter" wasn't the standard version of southern diners: an oversized oval with an overcooked country ham steak swimming in bitter, badly made red-eye gravy. (Is red-eye gravy ever good?) The Garage Bar's platter was served on a pressed metal circle bearing small, pink ribbons of thinly sliced, aged country ham from three area ham producers. Those hams—sliced only to order, never in bulk and never cooked—were just as outstanding as Newsom's. It didn't hurt a bit that those meats were paired with a clever red-eye aioli and thin slices of artisan baguette.

It turned out that Garage Bar wasn't the only restaurant in town serving country ham as charcuterie. Several local chefs had done it secretly for some time, curing pork in their restaurants' HVAC rooms or walk-in refrigerators and adding slices to special guests' plates. Bob Hancock—a co-owner, artisan baker and chef at Louisville's Blue Dog Bakery—was not only curing his own hams, he was also raising a small drove of Red Wattle pigs on a farm in Goshen, Kentucky, a Louisville exurb. For some time, Hancock even held special "Red Hog Tapas Night" events centered on those cured meats. It was clear that even I, a restaurant reporter for two decades, had missed country ham's rise to the fine dining stage, and I wasn't a little embarrassed.

Fast-forward to 2013, when my friend Fred Minnick said that a publisher had approached him about writing a book on country ham. Minnick, a whiskey and wine writer, said that chronicling pork tales wasn't his strong suit but that he knew a writer who might be interested.

The publisher was The History Press in Charleston, South Carolina, and its commissioning editor, Kirsten Schofield, told me that she wanted an in-depth look at country ham as a southern treasure, a disappearing craft from the bygone days when a home refrigerator was a luxury item. Sixty years ago, curing meat was about avoiding wintertime starvation and less the creation of a savory centerpiece for a Christmas feast. We discussed the growing number of fine dining chefs using country ham not only in the South but also in restaurant hot spots such as New York City, Los Angeles and San Francisco. There they served it sliced as charcuterie, uncooked and unadorned. Clearly, this formerly unpretentious regional delicacy had grown into a good story.

Surprisingly, the story was unknown to many residents of the Country Ham Belt, including most longtime artisan curers. Outside upscale restaurants in Tennessee, Kentucky, Virginia, North Carolina and Missouri, few knew that the humble cured ham, the meat their ancestors made to survive, had outgrown its blasé biscuit-filler role to become a hot ticket in restaurants, where it was served on cold meat plates, wood-fired pizzas and pricey scallop appetizers. Some were amazed to learn that anyone would eat uncooked pork, no matter how cured—although, ironically, several admitted to enjoying prosciutto sliced for a cold sandwich. It was a tall order to convince them that the only difference between prosciutto and country ham was that the latter is smoked. I likely convinced no one in the cooked-only crowd that uncooked was really good and arguably better. About eating it just cured, one ham maker said to me, "That's just creepy to think about."

But Newsom knew better. Although an admitted fan of "lightly fried" country ham, she told me, "I sent you that package just to eat, figuring you'd not cook it because you used to be a chef. Chefs understand what this is, and they deserve a lot of credit for it becoming so popular. …Not everybody likes it that way, and that's OK. But eating it uncooked, like they do in Spain and Italy, is earning our hams here some respect over there and here, too. They liked my ham that way when I was over there, which makes me wonder how many people understand it that way here."

It's a question that arose often during my research for this book, a seven-month undertaking in which I drove more than two thousand miles across Kentucky and Tennessee to visit curers and the restaurants they supply. More often than not, the answer merely prompted another question: "Does it really matter whether people eat it cooked or uncooked?" As long as they're eating it, ham makers don't seem to mind. Sales are sales, and to each his own.

Disappointingly, the U.S. Department of Agriculture (USDA) isn't so keen on the consumption of uncooked country ham. Despite centuries of safe, successful ham curing the world over, the USDA recommends ham makers *not* market their products as ready to eat. Even Finchville Farms' Bill Robertson Jr., an unabashed fan of cooked ham, calls the USDA's concerns and warnings nonsense: "The product is shelf stable. If the guidelines we're given by the USDA to follow are correct, then there's no risk in eating that ham uncooked. Not only is it the damndest thing that they keep insisting on that when it's not necessary, I think it's hurting country ham's position in the marketplace. If country ham can't be eaten uncooked, but prosciutto can, how are we supposed to market against that?"

It's a good question, but hardly top of mind as Richard and I stack our heavily salted hams nested and with their hocks pointed in the opposite direction of those beside and above them (as advised by several curers). Layered this way for the first salting, each ham is rotated 180 degrees after the next salting to help the meat form into a desired teardrop shape. Stacking them atop one another helps push water and blood drawn out by the salt from the meat. It's sticky, gritty, messy work, but we like it, and we hope we do it right. We've spent about $300 this morning on fresh hams and cure and would like to eat our investment someday.

Within days, a pool of pink-tinted water has drained from the hams, out of the refrigerator and onto the garage floor. Since I live forty-five minutes from Richard's house, he's left to mop up the gooey mess by himself. Luckily for me, he's not one to complain about such things. But if he ever whines, I'll just blame Nancy Newsom. She started this whole thing anyway.

CHAPTER 1

COUNTRY HAM

A SOUTHERN CULTURE OF RAISING, KILLING, CURING AND CASHING IN

A Journey of Pork from Port to Fork

If there's a southerner alive who remembers life without pork, I'd like to meet him. He's either half the age of Methuselah or a victim of torturous seclusion at the hands of fervent vegans. To go anywhere in the South and not find pork on a plate, penned for fattening or cartoonishly rendered for advertising or amusement is nigh impossible. You simply can't miss it. It's everywhere. And thank God for that!

Pork is as essential to the Dixie diet as fried chicken, although the latter is enshrined as the region's iconic meal. According to Jeanne Voltz and Elaine Harvell's *The Country Ham Book*, hogs first came to our shores on the boats of Spanish explorer Hernando de Soto, who arrived in the early 1500s. Considering that transatlantic voyages could last a month, the thought of living below decks with hogs nearby is enough to get humans *and* pigs off their feed. But not even the risky uncertainty of a trip to the New World could separate a Spaniard from his swine, and again, for that we praise the Lord!

According to various accounts, the tale of curly tails trotting onto our beaches goes mostly like this. In 1539, De Soto led a fleet of ten ships carrying seven hundred men and about a dozen pigs to Florida's west coast. There the pigs did what wild animals do: invade, eat everything in sight and reproduce.

By the time De Soto left Florida a few years later—his ships surely covered with vulgar bumper stickers and stuffed with cheap T-shirts—their hog drove had grown to seven hundred. Although soaring real estate prices hadn't hit the land that one day would become the twenty-seventh U.S. state, the hogs were driven to Georgia, though not in DeSotos or any other powered vehicle. Even without spring break traffic choking the path north, the trip had to have been arduous. And just how do you move seven hundred hogs north en masse without some running off and starting families among the peach trees?

A few centuries would pass before the barbecue restaurant was invented, giving hogs time to figure out what to do until humans invented new ways to kill and eat them. So, the pigs reproduced in astounding numbers and migrated across the eastern United States. Unfortunately for them, they didn't consult with their travel agent before trotting to Virginia, where locals knew how to cure hams and bellies.

Like the aforementioned spring breakers, hogs made a general nuisance of themselves, and the Virginians wanted them dead, off their rudimentary lawns and turned into winter provisions and luggage. Naïvely confident of safety in numbers, the hogs apparently bought into the gossip among local animals that said that the settlers weren't skilled trappers. Of course, the hungry immigrants proved otherwise.

Winters were cold in Virginia, which made life harsh but provided perfect conditions for salt-curing the meat of feral pigs. Native Americans taught the settlers to smoke the pork for added flavor and preservation. With more hogs than the settlers could eat, there arose an opportunity to export ship-stable, salt-cured, smoked pork to other countries.

Clearly, the pigs' jig was up. Settlers fenced them in and ended their wandering ways. Like northerners who move to Florida to escape the cold but soon miss the changing seasons, the hogs probably pined for the land of wild orange groves, powdery beaches and warm breezes. What the pigs may have envisioned as hog heaven had become hog hell, particularly along the James River, where settlers proved to be skilled curers who had smartly positioned their operations near commercial waterways. By the 1900s, the riverside Virginia towns of Surry and Smithfield had become some of the busiest ham-curing sites in the New World.

Unfair as it seemed, such was the order of the food chain. Being fat, dumb and slow was a fine way to go through life except when confronted by hungry capitalists. Being slaughtered, salted, smoked and forked for a feast became commonplace for the descendants of De Soto's pigs. Their destiny was the dinner table, their terminus atop a pewter platter, glazed in maple and studded with cloves.

A Time to Kill

Despite the advent of small-scale commercial ham curing in the 1700s, the practice was mostly a family affair through to the 1940s, when curers began building mass-production plants. Most farmers killed hogs in cold weather, and some even followed lunar phases, believing that the meat was better if harvested under a full moon.

Of course, the effort was bereft of romance: Hogs fattened more than a year or two were killed either by gunshot or a blow from an axe, sledgehammer or a nearby heavy rock. The pig's jugular was cut, the blood was drained and then hot water was poured onto the animal's skin to help scrape off its coarse hair. (If you're tempted to skip this part of the book, remind yourself that this was a family affair, requiring the assistance of men, women and even children! So c'mon, tough it out and return to the kill site.)

Dead, bled and scalded, the animal was then hung upside down by its rear hooves and gutted. A butcher slit the hog from crotch to throat, taking care not to puncture its intestines—its unpalatable contents could ruin the flavor of and potentially contaminate the meat. The butcher—usually the man of the house—also wanted to preserve the intestines and internal organs for boiling, frying and sausage-making. People didn't slaughter hogs in the olden days just for the baby back ribs and a pair of pork tenderloins. They used every part of the animal, from "the rooter to the tooter," to maximize a precious resource and widen the wintertime menu.

Since hogs were slaughtered from late November through early February, the meat could remain in the smokehouse without spoiling. Much of it was salted, but just some parts were smoked. Many cuts, especially smaller ones, were consumed during winter. Larger portions, such as hams and shoulders, would be smoked in the spring when warm air relaxed the meat and allowed it to better absorb the flavors of smoldering hickory.

Since the whole family was on the job, everyone had a duty. Men typically managed the cutting, scalding and scraping, while women rendered fat pieces for lard in an iron kettle perched over a wood fire. They also salted the meat and reduced large pieces to smaller portions.

Believe it or not, a "hog killin'" was a festive event, when families and neighbors gathered to expedite the process and, hopefully, celebrate a plentiful harvest. The hog's internal organs and loins often were consumed that day as the group's reward.

My mother, Mary Ann Thompson, grew up in Mayfield, Kentucky, where hog killing typically commenced on Thanksgiving Day, when factory workers, such as her father, had the day off. That morning, my PaPa and an uncle or two would slaughter a hog and ready it for a winter respite in the smokehouse. A few cuts of fresh pork were set beside the roasted turkey as part of the Thanksgiving feast, and one of Mom's mischievous uncles insisted that the morning's harvest was still wiggling.

"We were little then, so it scared us some, but it also made us laugh," my mother said, recalling those 1950s holidays shared with seven siblings. "That was just part of Thanksgiving at our house. The best part was knowing Daddy was going to make sausage and country ham."

Fred Noe III, master bourbon distiller at Jim Beam in Clermont, Kentucky, learned to make whiskey and cure hams under the tutelage of his father, the legendary distiller Fred "Booker" Noe Jr. By the time Fred came along, the Noes didn't slaughter their own animals; they hired others to do it outside in a field for thirty dollars per pig. (The price hasn't risen much since Noe's childhood. In 2012, I paid eighty-four dollars for the same service at a butcher shop about two miles from Noe's home in Bardstown, Kentucky. If you've read this far, you know that it was eighty-four dollars well spent.)

"Curing hams is what my granddaddy and daddy did, and so we still do it today," said Noe. "We all still come up to the house, rub the hams with salt, have a few drinks, a few laughs, tell stories and have a good time. And all our hams still go in the smokehouse out back."

Noe recalled one fall when his father took a 685-pound sow to his slaughtering buddies. "Those guys looked at that sow and said, 'We haven't killed one that big in a long time!'" Noe said. "When Dad asked if they charged more, they said no, that it was the same. So Dad told me to get a few bottles of whiskey out of the truck to give to them, just to be friendly. I remember them asking him, 'Do you mind if we have a drink before we get started?' We didn't care, of course, but before long, they were lit up!"

The slaughter of his massive sow wasn't Booker's only challenge that day. Kentucky's notoriously fickle fall weather delivered a chilly morning

Left: Fred Noe, master distiller, Jim Beam.

Below: John T. Edge, director of the Southern Foodways Alliance. *Photo by Angie Mosier.*

that became a warm day and didn't cool off that night. Without a cold smokehouse in which to stash the carcass for later butchering, the Noes were in a pinch. They decided to bring the hog inside and finish breaking it down—on the dinner table—and then find refrigeration elsewhere. Booker's wife, Annis, was not pleased to see the colossal carcass in her dining room.

"There it was, in the middle of Jim Beam's house on my mother's dinner table," Fred Noe said. "My mother still talks about 'that damn hog in the middle of my table.' She'll never let me live that one down."

Writer John T. Edge is the director of the Southern Foodways Alliance, an institute of the Center for the Study of Southern Culture at the University of Mississippi. Edge is somewhat concerned that the old-time craft of curing country ham is disappearing because families can buy cured ham at the store. Although consumption remains fairly strong (about 2.5 million country hams are made annually in the United States), production has shifted mostly to large factories and professional curers.

"Country ham is what sustained working-class families for many generations, especially those in the upper South," Edge said. "Consumers still identify with the roots of that food as very much a subsistence activity, but that's not a bad thing. It's part of the South's rich history."

Ironically, Edge said, younger consumers and restaurant chefs seem most interested in retaining and reviving that part of southern culture, despite having few direct ties to farms where country hams were cured by families. "It has this kind of totemic good that represents a kind of unvarnished southern past," Edge noted. "Those chefs aren't a part of that past, but they want to be a part of it. They see the value in that connection."

Edge believes that the enthusiasm for traditionally southern food and drink could eventually spill over to country ham and accelerate its revival. "You can say that about a number of artisan products across number of disciplines in the South, that they have this new cachet, that they're popular again," Edge said. "We have this segment of the population that's learned to value traditional crafts, things like ham and bourbon. ...But what's interesting is to see how we have craft production and industrialization of the same things running parallel to each other. Despite mass production, you still have a deepening appreciation of the old ways. I see that as good for country ham."

In Need of Respect

The South, where country ham is well known and oft eaten, is the very place where it seems to garner the least respect—based on price tags, anyway. Go to any suburban supermarket or delicatessen and check the cost of imported prosciutto ham. Sliced for charcuterie, it can command anywhere from $15 per pound (for prosciutto di Parma) to $25 per pound (for prosciutto San Danieli). Spain's serrano ham will set you back $50 per pound, and the legendary *Ibérico* costs $100 per pound. By comparison, the cost of thin-sliced country ham aged a year or more ranges from $8 to $15 per pound. But the few curers who age their hams up to two years fetch between $35 and $55 per pound, depending on the brand.

An increasing number of restaurants in the South do slice country ham for charcuterie, but that presentation is most often featured elsewhere in the United States. That irony isn't lost on Peter Kaminsky, author of *Pig Perfect* and a cured ham devotee who has traveled the world pursuing his passion for pork. Kaminsky said that non-southerners don't view country ham as

a blue-collar staple or a holiday dish. It's simply cured ham and delicious, so they consider it similar to prosciutto or serrano. "There's no great ham-making tradition in the rest of the country, so country ham is a southern thing," Kaminsky said. Still, he believes that is changing. "You didn't see it around in restaurants fifteen years ago, but ever since, the farm-to-table movement has helped country ham."

Fatty, rich slices of Woodlands Pork Mountain ham.

Gregg Rentfrow, PhD, associate extension professor of Meat Science at the University of Kentucky's Department of Animal and Food Science, said that chefs outside the South are driving the growth in country ham consumption. He noted that chefs are always looking for unique treats, and now, many want salt-cured, smoked ham. "It's one thing to say they want just country ham, but they'll say they want it from pigs of a heritage breed that most of us don't see much anymore," Rentfrow said. "They're looking for that edge, something that makes their menu stand out as different—not just the guys making thirty thousand hams a year, sometimes the people making only six hundred hams a year."

Adisa Kalkan said that she sees country ham gaining that edge in restaurants and supermarket prepared foods sections. As the manager of marketing and research and development at Volpi Foods, a St. Louis, Missouri-based maker of prosciutto and Italian salumi, Kalkan visits grocery stores in search of cured meat trends. She said that the country hams of smaller producers are benefitting from the growing number of chefs recognizing their quality as equal to European hams. "But what I think is really interesting is to see the crossover attention that prosciutto is getting from and giving to country ham," added Kalkan. "People are recognizing that the quality of country ham is really good and that it's so much like prosciutto."

Kalkan said that slicing country ham for charcuterie—with its fat on— would do wonders for the product when presented to old-world charcuterie purists. "Cutting that good fat off of an aged ham is like taking the bubbles out of champagne," she said. "You cut it off in Italy, and they'll yell at you. You have to leave it. It's so good!"

Bill Robertson Jr., former owner of Finchville Farms Country Ham in Finchville, Kentucky, said that the country ham industry has become its own worst enemy by choosing to compete on price. As a result, the industry commoditized its core product. "It's no longer seen as the delicacy it once was," Robertson said. "It's become all about the damn price, and less so about the quality. There used to be so many good small country ham makers just about everywhere you went, but there was no way they could compete against larger operations like ours. So when those guys quit producing hams, nobody followed them into the business."

Industrial-scale pork production also has removed noticeable flavor differences in pork. To ensure retailer demands for product consistency, genetically similar pigs are fed similar diets and confined to industrial facilities for feeding and farrowing. Each animal is tracked from birth to

Bill Robertson Jr., former owner, Finchville Farms Country Hams.

slaughter by a microchip attached to its ear, allowing producers to raise consistently lean hogs that yield supermarket-ready cuts in the most cost-effective fashion.

Fans of European hams usually know that their pork comes from animals specifically bred and fed to produce fattier, more flavorful meat. American hams won't have the same cachet, Kaminsky said, until American producers make the same investment in high-quality hogs and feed. "For us to be able to have ham command the price that will make it worthwhile for farmers to produce raise optimal pork, things have to change," Kaminsky said.

The problem is that heritage-breed, free-range hogs are hard to find. "There just aren't enough people raising them," said Sam Edwards III, president of S. Wallace Edwards & Sons Country Hams in Surry, Virginia. "We know better pork makes a better ham, but getting your hands on it is another matter."

Comparisons Don't Matter

Kaminsky warned not to compare American country hams to hindquarters cured elsewhere in the world because no ham is definitively better than another. They're just different, he said, and uniqueness should be celebrated, not criticized. It's vital, he said, to allow the hams of different countries and regions to express their unique *terroir*, a French term describing the influence of geography, geology and climate on indigenous plants and animals. "Where's the fun in having all hams taste the same way?" he said. "If we eat them for their flavor, we want things to be unique."

Edge suspects that southerners have a slight inferiority complex, even amid the blooming appreciation of their native food and drink. Polenta, for example, has long enjoyed a spot on pricey menus at fine Italian restaurants, but southern grits are regarded homely by comparison. "It's taken America some time to understand that our grits made well and served on our soil…kick polenta's arse all day long, but now we're getting it," Edge said. "Now you see the respect grits have gotten in restaurants, so the framing is important."

Rentfrow agreed: "Whether people here care to admit it or not, food is part of a regional identity. Just ask barbecue guys. They are serious about it. In the same way, Kentucky is known for country ham and bourbon, and those are great things."

To see how well country ham is respected in other American cities, travel to the nation's dining capitals and peruse better menus. Several years ago, Edge joined Allan and Sharon Benton, owners of Benton's Smoky Mountain Country Hams, on a trip to New York City to visit some highly respected chefs using Benton's products.

"When you see David Chang [chef-owner of Momufuku Restaurant Group] genuflecting in Allan's presence, or when you go to Bobby Flay's restaurant, where they deified Allan, you begin to see just how important that ham and that man are to those chefs," Edge said. "It took those chefs to reframe that ham and bacon as a full-bore country boy product worthy of a white tablecloth. They showed America the value of those products by reframing them as artisanal. That was a transformative moment that happened ten or so years back."

Feed It to the Kids

When Robertson got into the business in the late 1960s, whole hams made up the bulk of Finchville Farms' sales. But families are smaller now and less inclined to cook at home, so consumers want prepackaged products in small portions. The buy only what they need and what's ready to eat.

Chain restaurants, especially fast-food brands, want much the same: prepackaged elements that can be cooked quickly and served on a platter with eggs or stuffed between biscuit halves. A generation ago, restaurants did the portioning; now producers do it for them.

The opposite is happening in pricier restaurants, where chefs buy whole hams from which they serve paper-thin charcuterie carved to order. It's that experience, Kaminsky said, that will tell the story of American country ham to the mouths of diners, especially in restaurants where it's served alongside European hams. He believes that younger diners will help drive this trend because they've been trained to seek the best food at restaurants rather than prepare them at home. "People are starting to appreciate it, [and when they] go to a restaurant, they want it sliced; they don't want it cooked," Kaminsky said. For optimal flavor and presentation, "thin-sliced ham should be served *a la minute*, as it were."

Edge shares Kaminsky's hope that country ham will get its due as diners search for more interesting food experiences, especially those rooted in America's past. But he would hate to see country ham become a status-conscious choice of the self-appointed cognoscenti. "Those are bullshit *poseur* stances," Edge said, "a gastronome taking on airs."

Although Edge celebrates the growing acceptance of country ham, he's concerned that it could become too popular. Much like NASCAR has alienated its historically blue-collar fan base by constantly hiking ticket prices, Edge worries that country ham could become unattainable to its traditional customers. "[If] it becomes gentrified and priced to the point where working-class southerners can't afford to eat it, that's a failure," Edge said. "If that becomes the same future for things like barbecue or all other traditional southern foods, that's a big step in the wrong direction."

Still, some modernizing of the cycle of country ham making would benefit the craft, Edge noted. If more small producers became vertically integrated by raising their own heritage breed pigs and processing and curing their meat, the cycle of farrowing to curing would be locally centralized instead of broadly industrialized.

As demonstrated by the explosion of farmers' markets across the country, local foods are increasingly important to food-conscious folk who want boutique products for their perceived purity and quality. Restaurants especially want dependable, high-quality pork sources that raise animals humanely, don't use antibiotics unnecessarily and feed those pigs all-natural diets. A large and vocal contingent of southern chefs already are championing such pork as better tasting, and they're marketing that commitment to better sourcing on their menus to raise customer awareness.

"The guys at Jim and Nick's [Community Bar-B-Q] are working with Cochon [restaurant] in New Orleans to raise heirloom pigs and run their own processing plant," Edge said. "It's a small start, but it's a start. It's vertical integration at its simplest: raise pigs, slaughter them and make your own ham."

CHAPTER 2

HAM IT UP!

COUNTRY HAM FESTIVALS

Ham festivals are fall festivals typically held during the month-long gap between the end of the crop harvest and the once-traditional beginning of the pork harvest. It's at this point on the calendar that the flavor and texture of country hams achieve a mostly equal balance of tastiness and tenderness. Most hams are eight to ten months old, still tender, fairly moist—no longer spongy—and highly flavorful after the hot and humid summer sweat.

Most southerners would call them perfect since they cook their country ham and because any remaining moisture helps maintain tenderness. Those who like them sliced for uncooked consumption will continue aging their hams six to twelve months longer to develop even more intense and complex flavors. Either way, such a long wait for something so delicious is indeed a good reason for a party.

There are three major country ham festivals in the South: Ham Days in Lebanon, Kentucky (late September); Trigg County Country Ham Festival in Cadiz, Kentucky (mid-October); and Spring Hill Country Ham Festival in Spring Hill, Tennessee (early October). With the passing years, all three have grown substantially and become events less about country ham and more about displays of crafts, carnival foods, rides and the sale of many things unrelated to cured pork. Since good parties nearly always grow, that expansion in scope is neither unexpected nor bemoaned.

Festivals are still fun. They draw huge crowds and give locals within a cluster of nearby counties one last chance to be cordial before the start of high school football playoffs. Here's a glimpse into the culture of Kentucky's two festivals.

Ham Days, Lebanon, Kentucky

It doesn't take a lot of skill to find the kitchen where the Ham Days country ham breakfast is prepared. There's no breeze on this warm fall morning to scatter the scents of frying ham and baking biscuits, yet even if there were a wind, you could still rely on your ears to hear the volunteer kitchen crew of about a dozen men laughing and clanging perforated spatulas as they work.

Inside the balmy kitchen, the crew is gathered around a bank of commercial stoves cooking country ham slices in deep pans of boiling lard. Nearby, another pair cooks down a massive pan of red-eye gravy, which, in the traditional, starch-thickened sense, is not gravy at all. To their pan of ham drippings, they add sugar and water and reduce the mixture to a black, unctuous-sweet anti-gravy that resembles used motor oil. "I can't tell you how we make it," Bruce Higdon jokes, "because it's an ancient Chinese secret."

When one man stirs their mixture too vigorously and splashes drippings onto the gas-flame burner, a hissing and sizable flare-up follows. Instinctively, the men on the ham frying line spin around to see the unscripted conflagration and watch their friends extinguish it. Soon, as they surmise that the flames are under control, the ham fryers start heckling the gravy makers.

"You're going to burn us down, boys! That's a hard way to get out of working today," says one heckler. Seeing me scribbling some notes, he points toward me and says, smiling, "Now, don't you write that down in your book; we're all friends here. This is how we have a good time with each other. It's all in fun."

When I ask to meet the volunteer coordinator, several fingers point—almost accusingly—to Robert Shewmaker, a veteran of the Ham Days kitchen. Briefly feigning reluctance to be interviewed, Shewmaker turns loquacious and says, "I really go by Darrell, so don't listen to them when they call me Robert." Wearing a red ball cap from Ham Days 2003, Shewmaker declares that this is his fortieth year on duty (the festival is now in its forty-fifth year) and then jokes that he really doesn't belong here.

Slices of ham cooking in lard at Ham Days.

Forty-year volunteer Darrel Shewmaker (center) laughs it up at Ham Days.

"I'm not a real cook. I'm just a country boy who knows how to kill and cook hogs," he says. When a volunteer in the background says, "Watch him wind up! Here he goes," Shewmaker smiles and ignores him. "I've been doing this so long because I like it," says Shewmaker, seventy-six, turning back toward his friends. "These guys act like they're working, too, but they're just having fun. This is a tight-knit community who comes in and helps if you ask."

Shewmaker's crew began working at 5:30 a.m., cooking 2,500 of the 5,000 pounds of country ham to be consumed over the event's two days. (Ham Days attracts about thirty thousand people per year.) Outside, volunteers heat pots of stewed apples over knee-high propane burners, while a pair at another post scrambles eggs in batches for transport to a buffet line.

As his helpers cut open vacuum-sealed packages of sliced ham, Shewmaker recalls the early years of Ham Days, when cooks worked with whole hams, removing their rinds and bones before cutting thousands of slices with a meat saw. "Oh, it's changed a bunch since then! There ain't much to it but cooking it now," Shewmaker says. "Of course, we were feeding only 1,500 back then, so that part was easier, but you still had to do it all. We did that for four nights to get ready." Scanning the kitchen, Shewmaker spies Randy Mattingly, another veteran cook, and says, "I'm fixing to quit this, though. This might be my last one. Randy is taking over."

"Oh, I don't know about that. Where else would you go, Darrell?" says Mattingly, grinning. "I know Ham Days isn't what it used to be. It's changed. But it does acknowledge our heritage, which is important."

Like Shewmaker, the sixty-one-year-old Mattingly grew up on a farm killing hogs, curing hams, making lard, raising beef cattle, chickens and a large garden. "We were feeding our family with all that," he recalls. "When you went to the store, it was only for the bare necessities of sugar and flour."

Shewmaker says that each day's shift cooking and cleaning will last about eight hours. Acknowledging the morning's ideal weather, he adds, "It's a long day in here when it gets hot, and we've had years when we came in wearing short britches. Other years, we had to wear a jacket. And it's just awful when it rains, but that hasn't happened too much."

About a block from the kitchen, nine hundred runners stream down Main Street toward the finish line of the Pokey Pig race. It's a 5K sprint for some, a leisurely walk for others and perhaps a silly dare for others dashing by in skirts and costumes. Reminding the crowd of their toughness, several firefighters complete the race in their fireproof overcoats and pants. Stripping off their heavy coats at the finish line reveals their sweat-soaked T-shirts. The Jr.

Local firemen
run in the
Pokey Pig 5K in
full gear.

Farmer and Little Miss Ham Days contest is next, followed by a Children's
Parade, a hog-calling contest and a country ham auction.

One block up Proctor Knott Avenue, a crowd of about two hundred sits
in folding chairs around picnic tables carving up country ham, biscuits, eggs
and apples with plastic utensils. (Few, it appears, accept the volunteers' offer
of the red-eye gravy.) The hearty meal costs eight dollars.

One couple from Louisville, David and Joyce Lange, made the ninety-
minute drive south with David's parents to see the event firsthand. A traveling
salesman for a large coffee wholesaler, Lange spends a lot of time in small
towns servicing accounts, but he says that he regrets lacking the time to
stay longer in towns like Lebanon. "Isn't this nice, the way they do this?"

Lange says, gesturing broadly toward the scene. "I love the city, but there's something about small towns—they just give you a good feeling. You wouldn't see this in a city."

Trigg County Country Ham Festival

Fans of small-town country events would have loved the first Trigg County Country Ham Festival. Some would argue that it was exactly as such festivals should be: small, intimate, a little silly, always friendly and all about country.

According to hamfestival.com, the inaugural event was held in downtown Cadiz, Kentucky, in 1977. There were thirty merchant booths, a country ham contest, a square dance, a rocking chair marathon, a greased pig catching competition and a tricycle race involving some public officials who had to chew tobacco—and not spit—during the entire race. Perhaps not surprisingly, the Old Fashioned Hog Killing Display didn't survive into the second year. Even country folk, it appeared, considered live hog slaughtering a bit too authentic even for a ham heritage festival.

That humble beginning quickly gave way to much larger spectacles. By 1982, booth numbers had doubled to seventy, and the festival had added a parade. In 1985, when fifteen thousand people attended the festival, volunteers set out to bake the world's largest country ham and biscuit: the finished product weighed four hundred pounds. (The *Guinness Book of World Records* never confirmed Trigg County's record claim. Smithfield, Virginia, another town with a rich ham heritage, did have its largest ham biscuit claim certified by Guinness in 2003.)

By 2013, booth count had grown to 170, in addition to a car show, a petting zoo, carnival rides, a golf tournament, canning and preserving contests, multiple concerts and musical acts, three beauty pageants and much more. Although the website says that the ham show and judging "continue to be a focal point of the Saturday activities," during my visit, not many from the already large crowd stopped to eyeball the two dozen hams laid out for judging under the small Kentucky Farm Bureau tent.

"We never really know how many will be in the contest until the day comes," says Janeen Tramble. She helps coordinate the contest through her work with the 4-H Country Ham Project, which teaches kids to cure hams. In years past, as many as forty hams were entered in the contest, but Tramble believes that this

Welcome to Cadiz, Kentucky, home of the Trigg County Country Ham Festival.

year's haul of half that reflects the gradual decline of the craft. "So many of our older ham makers have passed away, and no one in their family is carrying on that tradition. People aren't curing like they used to since they can just buy it."

Regardless of entry numbers, Alan Watts, news director at FM radio station WKDZ, dutifully reports live from the event, talking to ham makers, contest competitors, exhibitors, organizers and attendees. "We do this every year," Watts says, sweating a bit on the unseasonably warm October morning. "It's the biggest event all year in Cadiz, and everyone comes together. Everyone and then some!" He isn't exaggerating. The Ham Festival estimates crowd attendance at about 55,000, for Friday, Saturday and Sunday. That's more than twenty times the number of Cadiz residents, according to the U.S. Census Bureau's 2012 count of 2,609.

By midmorning Saturday, a sun-splashed crowd of several thousand surges slowly down Main Street, buying trinkets, candy and the usual starchy-greasy carnival food. Their cooking produces aromas of caramelized sugar and overworked deep fryers that linger on the skin. A few people stop to peak at the contest hams and wonder aloud why Katelyn Hawkins is sticking them with an ice pick. The graduate student in Meat Science Department at the University of Kentucky (UK) College of Agriculture is the contest's lone judge.

"The first thing I'm looking at is muscle confirmation, then color and then to see if they have that teardrop shape that's so traditional," said Hawkins, whose graduate position is meats coach. There are two categories: one for the 4-H kids' hams and another for adults who don't cure commercially. None of the adults' entries has the aforementioned teardrop shape: some are elongated and others quite flat, with their coloring ranging from mahogany to burnt sienna. Few of the adult hams bear the pecan color commonly seen in commercially produced hams. All the 4-H hams do since they were produced with help from Broadbent's B&B Foods.

I ask Hawkins if it matters whether the adult entries aren't teardrop shaped, and she says no. Such hams mirror those cured by individual families for centuries. "In a way they're kind of cool, except for that one. That ham's too dark for me. But most of your points come from your aroma anyway."

Shoving the ice pick into a space near the hip socket of a ham, she gives an impromptu anatomy lesson about a large vein that feeds that muscle area. If the pig's blood isn't squeezed out from that vein prior to curing, she says, any liquid remaining will produce a musty odor that results in a points deduction. "What I'm looking to smell is a little bit of spice, a little pepper edge and a little sweetness mixed in," Hawkins says. "It can be overly sugared, too, and if the aroma's kind of flat, those are points off, too."

She sticks the pick into another ham and holds it out for me to smell. "See, you can smell little notes of smoke and pepper in there. I try to think of a

Katelyn Hawkins, graduate student of University of Kentucky, judges the 2013 ham contest.

brown sugar ham to see if I can find sweetness. Not caramelized sugar, but sort of diluted brown sugar."

Meanwhile, I'm asked to be the third judge in a country ham biscuit contest. Seven entries are placed before us one at a time, including a delicious sweet potato biscuit with ham. We all like the unusual presentation and remark with smiles and nods. But we settle on a more traditional ham biscuit, one that's slightly dense, gently beaten and with a granulated texture wholly different from pastry-like grocery store biscuits. "This is just good, really good," one judge whispers among us. "I don't need to try to describe it in detail in front of a food writer, so I'll just say it's the best of the bunch." He's right. It is.

The biscuits were made by Belinda Holland, a bubbly, curly-haired woman in a red-checked blouse. As she's presented with a plaque for her win, Watts moves in to do a live radio interview. (See the recipe for Belinda's Buttermilk Biscuits in the recipes chapter.) Standing by is her husband, Tony Holland, who has a ham entered in this year's contest. He's won it twice and thinks he's got a good chance for a third grand champion ham. "This is my eighth year [in the contest], but it doesn't matter a lot whether I win it," Holland says. "I just really enjoy curing hams."

After several years living in Frankfort, Kentucky, while working as a state bridge inspector, he and his wife returned to Cadiz eager to plant a large garden, to can much of its yield "and to start curing our own hams. We do let someone else do the hog killing for us, but we cut it up ourselves. It's a fun day."

Holland ages his hams at least eleven months but says that he's begun holding over at least one ham from each sixteen-ham batch for a second year of aging. He says that fattier hams are best for extended aging. "Myyyyy *Lord*, the last one I tasted was unbelievable, probably the best thing I've ever put in my mouth," he says, adding that he lets them hang in a dark corner of his basement for twenty-four months. Asked to describe its taste, he says with a grin, "I don't know how to describe it. All I taste is fine eating."

While Hawkins continues probing contestants' hams and scribbling scores, Tramble introduces me to Robert Wadlington, son of a local ham curing legend, Charlie Bell Wadlington, now deceased. "I can't say I'm exactly sure why my father's hams were so good," says the soft-spoken Wadlington, who cures about 125 hams a year, the same number cured by his dad. "Maybe it was the way we cured it or how he smoked it with hickory sawdust and aged it for nine or ten months."

The Wadlingtons used to raise and slaughter all their own hogs, hard work that Robert says he misses. "We'd kill them in the middle of December and through the middle of January," says the former row crop farmer who now works in construction. "It was something to do every day for three months, something different from being in the fields. …We'd shoot them in the head, scald them in a bath, get the hair off, gut them and then break it down to all the parts. We cured the hams, but we sold all the parts."

His hams are ambient cured, without refrigeration, but he places fans inside the smokehouse during the summer to circulate the air. To keep bugs under control, he sprinkles pepper all around and hangs multiple fly strips. "My hams are ready in eight to nine months, but you can keep them two years and they're still good," Wadlington says. "Every time they go through the sweat stage, it changes the flavor, improves it. But I don't like mine too hard."

Both Wadlington and Holland have taught their daughters to cure hams, and both say that each has an excellent nose for assessing aging. Wadlington's wife, Laura, says that their daughter is a two-time 4-H grand champion. "She's enjoyed doing it, which really shocked me," she said. "There are lots of girls involved in the [4-H] country ham program. And I think that might be because they like being with their dads."

Earlier that morning, Sarah Shipley also told me that there are more girls than boys in the 4-H program. "Hey, you'd be surprised how many girls are

Laura and Robert Wadlington, local ham curers.

in the program," she says, answering my shocked expression and sticking up for her gal pals. The Trigg County High School junior has cured hams for six years. "You cure two hams each year: one goes to the state fair, and the other you take home and cook. This one I'm holding got a blue ribbon at the state fair."

In 4-H contests, only 40 percent of a student ham maker's score is based on the finished meat; 60 percent comes from each curer's ability to give a three- to five-minute speech on a subject related to ham making. "Mine was on the parasites that can get into country ham," she says. "They want us to learn more than just how to cure."

Left: Student competitor Sarah Shipley shows a ham that won her a blue ribbon at the Kentucky State Fair.

Below: Alan Watts, news director for WKDZ in Cadiz, interviews ham contest winner Tony Holland. His wife, Belinda, who won the ham biscuit competition earlier, looks on.

With her ham evaluations completed, Hawkins turns in her score sheets for tabulation, takes off her apron and prepares for the five-hour drive back to UK. She'd made the drive here just this morning. "Am I tired? Not really," Hawkins says. "This contest is nothing compared to the state fair. When you see seven hundred country hams in once place—and those are just the students' hams—it's an eye-opener."

Although not a judge, Ronnie Drennan, co-owner of Broadbent's B&B Foods, a ham curer in Kuttawa, Kentucky, did his own ice picking and prodding of several hams yet reserved his remarks so as to not influence Hawkins's opinion. "Judging a ham is like judging a beauty contest: it's a lot about what *you* like," Drennan says. Not only did Drennan help the bulk of the 4-H kids from western Kentucky produce their state fair hams, he's also had a few grand champions of his own, including the legendary $1.6 million ham auctioned off in 2010. "There's really not a bad ham here today, only some that might be better in some ways than others."

When the ribbons are handed out, Tony Holland's ham is the grand champion. Out of nowhere comes Watts, microphone in hand, for an interview of the winner. As Holland shares some curing techniques on live radio, his wife, Belinda, stands beside him beaming, surely considering the day's all-Holland sweep. When Watts finishes, Holland tells me that he sells some of his hams for $100 each, a fee friends call too low. His standard response is that he doesn't cure hams for money. "People say I should charge more and go into business doing it, but then it wouldn't be fun anymore," he says. "It's just something I love, and part of why is seeing that happy face when people taste it. To get a text saying, 'That was even better than last year,' that makes you feel good when you produce something like that."

Later that afternoon, I meet Smith Broadbent III to chat about his time as a ham curer. In the course of our conversation, he asks if I'd seen the giant biscuit.

"What?" I ask.

"The big country ham biscuit. It was the world's largest," he replies. Still unclear on what he meant, Broadbent produces a photocopy of a recipe typed in 1995 for a ten-foot-wide biscuit weighing 400 pounds. In addition to the 150 pounds of flour and 39 pounds of shortening required to make it, the behemoth biscuit is cut into nine hundred portions and filled with slices from sixteen of Broadbent's country hams.

"So you didn't get to see it or taste any of it?" Smith's wife, Katie Broadbent, asks. Their expressions tell me that I'd missed what arguably is the festival's pièce de résistance. I reply sheepishly, "No, ma'am, I didn't.

I was down at the ham contest all morning, and I didn't think to leave. I somehow missed that."

In a conciliatory tone, she says, "You can always come back next year. They'll do it again." I read the recipe again and am amazed at the oven used to make the biscuit. The baking surface is 576 cubic feet, requires multiple handmade burners, has a total of 500,000 BTU output and weighs seven thousand pounds. A forklift is required to remove the gigantic biscuit.

"Who made this oven?" I ask.

"I did," says Broadbent. Despite battling Parkinson's disease, he still works his large farm in Cadiz at age seventy-one. Like many farmers, he's creative and industrious.

"You did?" I ask, and he nods and grins. "I think I'll come back next year just to see that oven!"

The Priciest Country Ham Auction in the United States: The Kentucky State Fair

Since 1964, the Kentucky State Fair has held forty-nine country ham contests, each of which is followed by a sale of the grand champion at the annual Kentucky Country Ham Breakfast & Auction. Among the breakfast's 1,600 attendees, about six dozen are local, state and national elected officials who turn out to speak, eat, poll the electorate and likely avoid their opponents in order to keep the peace. Unlike at the legendary Fancy Farm Picnic, an old-fashioned political stump-fest held every August in Fancy Farm, Kentucky, there's no fiery rhetoric or fightin' words allowed at the ham breakfast.

Perhaps the genteel mood set by those unwritten rules helps to ensure that attendees properly digest their enormous breakfasts. According to event sponsor Kentucky Farm Bureau, more than 5,400 eggs, 1,600 half-pints of milk, 30 gallons of sorghum, 20 gallons of honey, 6,400 oranges and 450 pounds of country ham are served that morning.

At the conclusion of this protein-packed feed, a countrified chow down that would have made Dr. Robert Atkins right proud, the state fair grand champion ham is placed on a silver platter, surrounded by roses, draped with the long purple winner's ribbon and presented to bidders by that year's Miss Kentucky. It's an ironically majestic finale for a hind end that spent

Jessica Casebolt, Miss Kentucky 2012, walks the grand champion ham before the bidders. *Courtesy of Kentucky Farm Bureau.*

many of its days ignobly covered in mud. Proceeds from the auction go to the bidder's (and oftentimes, bidders') chosen charities. According to the Kentucky Farm Bureau, the auction has helped raise $6.5 million for local charities, including educational institutions and philanthropic groups.

At the 1964 inaugural auction, the winning bid was $124 (about $932 in 2014 dollars). The record price for a grand champion is $1.6 million, paid in 2010 ($227,465 in 1964 dollars) for a ham produced by Broadbent's B&B Foods. Commonly known as Broadbent's, the ham curer is the winningest competitor in the contest's history, claiming fourteen grand champions—an overall win rate of 28.5 percent.

HAM EXCLUSIV

{ **50-year history of the KFB Kentucky Country Ham Breakfast & /**
Every year since 1964, Kentucky Farm Bureau has hosted a breakfa
agricultural heritage. Each year has also featured a high-energy auct
toward the charity or charities of the winning bidder's choice. Here

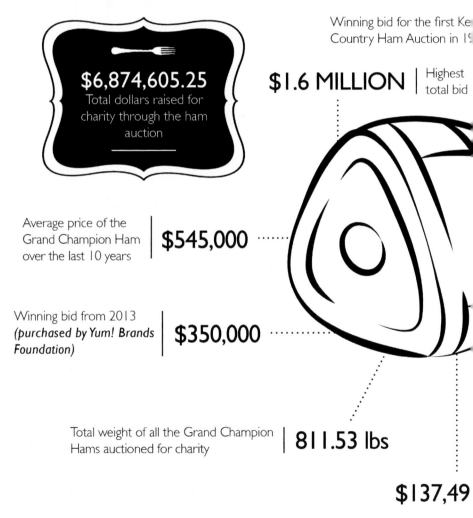

$6,874,605.25
Total dollars raised for
charity through the ham
auction

Winning bid for the first Ke
Country Ham Auction in 19

$1.6 MILLION | Highest
total bid

Average price of the
Grand Champion Ham
over the last 10 years | **$545,000**

Winning bid from 2013
(purchased by Yum! Brands
Foundation) | **$350,000**

Total weight of all the Grand Champion
Hams auctioned for charity | **811.53 lbs**

$137,49

Kentucky Country Ham
BREAKFAST

ntucky State Fair to celebrate our state's great
rized Grand Champion Ham with the proceeds going
ide the numbers of the Ham Auction's storied history…

}

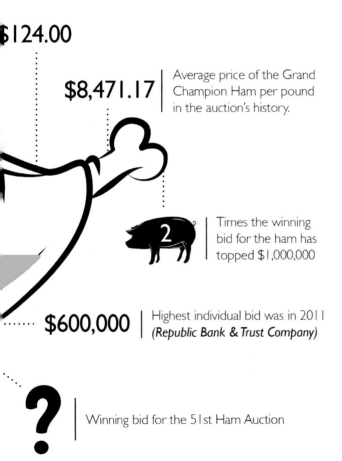

$124.00

$8,471.17 | Average price of the Grand
Champion Ham per pound
in the auction's history.

2 | Times the winning
bid for the ham has
topped $1,000,000

$600,000 | Highest individual bid was in 2011
(Republic Bank & Trust Company)

? | Winning bid for the 51st Ham Auction

verage price of the Grand Champion
lam in the auction's history

A look at the average
auction price paid for
the Kentucky State
Fair's grand champion
ham. *Courtesy of Kentucky
Farm Bureau.*

Over the past ten years, the average auction price has been $535,000, including 2013's $350,000 winning bid for a hindquarter from Harper's Country Hams in Clinton, Kentucky. While that number may sound small compared to Broadbent's $1.6 million ham, the Kentucky Farm Bureau says that it's the fourth-highest offer ever from a single bidder and the fifth-highest bid in the auction's history. The second-highest price for a state fair ham was 2009's $1.3 million bid. That came from four-time state fair grand champion Scott Hams in Greenville, Kentucky.

Both million-dollar bids were made up of collective bids from owners and operators of some of Louisville's largest and most prestigious companies. Among the record bidders are father and son Bernard and Steve Trager, past and current chairman, respectively, of Republic Bank.

According to Steve Trager, the bank donates its part of the purchase price to a range of education- and healthcare-related charities. In some years, it has created smaller secondary fundraisers by taking the winning ham, slicing it, turning it into sandwiches and selling those to raise even more charitable funds. "And sometimes we'll slice it and serve it for breakfast to our associates here at Republic," he said. "We've had some success at Republic, and this is part of what we do to give back to the community."

While ham-making contestants receive none of those lucrative proceeds, all insist that state fair wins produce a powerful PR punch. "There's nothing like saying yours was the grand champion," said Scott Hams' Leslie Scott. "That makes you fairly proud, and people pay more attention to you."

CHAPTER 3
MASTERS OF THE CRAFT

THE HAM MAKERS

Col. Bill Newsom's Aged Kentucky Country Ham
Princeton, Kentucky

Fine dining chefs have little time outside their kitchens, but at least a few times a year, several make personal visits to Col. Bill Newsom's Aged Kentucky Country Ham store in Princeton, Kentucky, about a three-hour drive from Louisville, Kentucky; Nashville, Tennessee; and St. Louis. Their pilgrimage is to see ham maker Nancy Newsom (the craftswoman dubbed "The Ham Lady" in her marketing materials) behind the sublime, aged hams made in her ambient-temperature curing houses. They want to know her ham secrets—how they're made, the reasons for their complex flavors, whether terroir *matters as much in pork curing as winemaking and more.*

Newsom demurs gently when asked such specifics, smiling and saying that the only people who will ever know are those willing to work with her or buy her business. Not that it's for sale yet, although she's fielded proposals. At age fifty-eight, Newsom is far from retirement, "but this old girl can only do this for so long," she says, grinning. When it's time to hand over her business, it'll be to someone she's mentored at length, someone who understands that ham aging cannot be rushed and who respects the centuries-old techniques she'll share. Not surprisingly, she believes, it'll be a chef.

If it gets to climate change making it impossible to cure hams the way I do it, I don't want this business anymore. I don't want to do climate-controlled. We let the weather control most of what we do. I don't have a problem with others who control the temperature in their ham houses; that's what they do. I do what my daddy taught me.

People look at what I do and say, "That's pretty simple. I think I can do that." But it takes so much time to learn this, and I've been at it a long time. I still learn something new every day. I can tell you the mechanics of the thing, but you have to see it for yourself and learn as you go.

I can't just tell you what to do when you face this or that weather condition. You have to see it to understand it. I can tell by touch when it's time to do the next thing. Like smoking: If it's damp, the hams won't take smoke as easily. If it's hot, it's easier. Overall, it takes weeks, and I can tell by the color they're taking on whether they've had enough. You've got to smell it, too. And you know, not everyone has the nose for this. There are only about two of us here who have a nose for checking hams.

My daddy ["Colonel" Bill Newsom] was so patient in teaching me. I guess I was about sixteen when I started. I was spoiled; he let me set my own hours, and he didn't demand I work in the business. I was pregnant with my first child when I really got involved in the mail-order side of it in 1983. In 1987, we had a fire at the general store…and I told Daddy that we really needed a place to sell the hams. He said, "Well, you do it, then," and I said I would. He was getting along in years and had a heart condition, and I wanted to carry that on for him.

I needed to know how he cured his hams, so I started asking questions: "How many pounds of salt did you use this time?" "How long until these come out of salt?" I got tidbits just a little at a time. His helpers accepted me pretty good, probably since I was with my dad a lot growing up and around them, too. An outsider might get a cold shoulder if he asked too many questions. [Ham makers] are very prideful of what they know how to do, so they don't always want any other dynamic in there. But they let me in there—maybe because I wasn't bad looking in that day, so they didn't mind me being around them! That's all I've got to say about that!

It is important to me that restaurant chefs choose our hams. We're proud of that. James Beard was the first chef to use our hams back in 1975, and he taught cooking lessons with them. He really launched our mail-order business through his writings about our hams. That was a blessing!

The appreciation for country ham is coming along slowly through chefs. They understand how special it is, that it's a dying art and that many of

Nancy Newsom in front of Colonel Bill Newsom's original smokehouse. *Photo by Anita Baker.*

Colonel Bill Newsom and Nancy Newsom. *Courtesy of Col. Bill Newsom's Aged Kentucky Country Hams.*

our hams are as good as those in Europe. We take the time to explain our processes to them and educate them. They get it.

Writers help, too. Peter Kaminsky—the guy who wrote *Pig Perfect*—he helped get us into the gourmet market. It was from his book and another one, [*Ham*]: *An Obsession with the Hindquarter*, that my ham was recognized internationally. It got me invited to Spain in 2009 [for the *Congreso Mundial del Jamón*, or World Congress of Ham]. To that time, I was the only American ham maker ever invited, and they loved my ham. One of my hams is hanging in Aracena [Spain, at the *Museo del Jamón*] now with other Spanish, Italian and German hams. Oh, Daddy would be proud! There's no other American producer with a ham there, and remember, a lot of these Spanish men are not used to a female producer.

AGED HAMS GET SO MUCH MORE RESPECT IN EUROPE THAN THEY DO HERE. In Spain, there's the *Ibérico* and the serrano and in Italy, the prosciutto. When I was in Spain, I saw how the Spaniards take such great pride in their hams that they hang them in their homes, in their bars and their restaurants; they love to show them off. One man took us down to his basement in his house just to show us his hams! They're as proud of those as we would be of a new car in the driveway.

The prices they get there are so high end! You see *Ibéricos* here for $1,500, and I'm selling my two-year-old hams for around $125. And I've got to tell you, our quality is as good! One time, I wasn't feeling well and couldn't travel to a food show in California. So Jay Denham [ham maker at Woodlands Pork] took my hams for me. And he said that Mario Batali's father came by the booth and tasted my ham, and he said it was $1,000 ham. I thought, oh my, that's good to know, but I don't think our nation is ready for that kind of pricing.

I charge $7.99 a pound for my [free-range] aged hams, but it really should be $8.99. People are always looking for higher-end things, but will they always pay it? That's debatable. But the people who will pay it are the types who don't spend money unwisely on other things. They have the money to do it already.

Some of my hams are from free-range pigs, but only a few hundred a year. People may say they want them, but they might change their plan as their income changes. Know what I'm saying? Price is a big deal to everybody. Me, too. I buy one lot of free-range hams for the same price I could have bought twice the number of the others. We put a pretty good cure on the factory-raised meat also, but not everyone has the palate to tell the difference anyway. There is a difference, though.

REGARDLESS, I TELL OTHER HAM MAKERS THEY NEED TO CHARGE MUCH MORE FOR THEIR HAMS AND THAT THEY COULD GET THAT PRICE. A lot are afraid that they'll lose long-term customers, and I understand that. But it's getting to where you can't make any money in this if you don't. What's dangerous is when you get to thinking that anybody *should* pay more for your product just because of the quality. All I have to say is you best be careful doing that.

But I know you asked me about my daddy. He was an interesting a man, a good man. He loved my mother [Jane Newsom]. He was highly independent, not going to kiss anybody's rear. If the president was waiting in line, he could wait. He cared about people like that, and he gave his all to his customers,

In the ham house with Nancy Newsom.

which is the tough part of retail businesses. People are always pulling on you, and you can lose yourself in it. They don't realize you're as busy as you are when you take time with them. I don't complain about that, though. I'm busy! When I get somebody on the phone, I'm grateful they call me.

Daddy could be funny, too. He used have lots of old sayings, like, "I'm busier than a stump full of ants." But he also was a man who said important things, like, "Each ham house has its own mold," which is so true. The particular molds in our smokehouses are very special, and I think it affects their flavor. When we opened our new smokehouse, we brought some hams from the old smokehouse, and that mold came with them.

Some people say they want a moldy ham, and others want us to take it off. Peter Kaminsky said [the mold on our hams] looked like a head on a beer! It's labor-intensive to get it off, but when you clean them and oil them up, it's the most beautiful mahogany—really pretty.

From the time we receive fresh hams until we sell them, we move each one eighteen times. [She produces eight thousand a year.] It's hard work that I don't think everybody would like to do, so I don't know who I'd sell it to. One day when I'm too old to run this, I think the right buyer will be a chef. They know how to work hard, and they don't expect everything to go smoothly. They know how to work scattered.

I had a guy from New York call me wanting to buy this from me, but I'm not ready to sell. He was very nice and told me he was all about trying to preserve a heritage, to not ruin something that was age-old and nostalgic. I have a son who helps some, but I don't know if he's interested enough to take over.

How do I like to eat my ham? Depends on whether I'm feeling my country side or I'm trying to feed my gourmet palate. You know what I'm getting at?

The other night, I fixed some homemade biscuits, and Herbert [her boyfriend] cooked it really nicely, caramelized just a little, and I could really taste that mystical flavor it gets from that old ham house. I really think my ham tastes best served as a prosciutto [sliced paper thin and served at room temperature]. But when those country hams are about a year old, soaked and boiled and still hot, pulling a piece out of the hock is about the best thing you ever ate.

I think part of why country ham is becoming more popular is people generally appreciate things that are hard to find. They also like knowing that the person who is making them loves doing it and will give them the best they've got. Anything that feels historical and laid-back, unique, nostalgic

The building housing Newsom's Old Mill Store is nearly 125 years old.

and comfortable—all these heritage and hand-crafted foods are connected to history, and people have a need to go back to them. Why do you think Ancestry.com is so popular today? Know what I'm getting at?

Also, part of that feeling is brought on by that missing [element of] service. Remember the day when people helped you put your shoes on your feet at the store? People want personalization again, and I see it in the way people order from us. They might order from the Internet the first time or two, but often the next time they call us. They want that connection.

IF YOU DON'T PUT ANY SOUL INTO WHAT YOU DO, THE CUSTOMER DOESN'T REALLY GET ANYTHING OUT OF IT. It used to be that you could fool the public about country hams—and they still do. But if you notice, the ones that are being highlighted more in the media are the ones that have held truer to the old ways, not those made faster and done quick. More and more, people are looking for artisanal foods because they see the value. I think that's why they like my ham.

Benton's Smoky Mountain Country Hams
Madisonville, Tennessee

Madisonville, Tennessee, is a tiny town in the western foothills of the Smoky Mountains, about forty miles southwest of Knoxville. It takes some effort to get there, but that doesn't stop folks from visiting regularly to buy one of Allan Benton's celebrated Smoky Mountain Country Hams.

Even at 8:30 a.m. on an icy November morning, a few customers are pulling into the small parking lot in front of Benton's modest green- and cream-colored cinder block building. Just a week before Thanksgiving, the official start of the Christmas selling season, a few hams hang at the edge of the building's awning, swaying in the chilly breeze.

Benton's office is as timeless as his ham making methods. His small desk is cluttered to the eye but apparently organized to his liking. A black rotary dial telephone, surely a half century old, sits on his desk, and its metal bells ring multiple times throughout our interview. Just once does the unceasingly courteous Benton halt the conversation to pick up the corded handset and talk. On a wall behind him are numerous business cards and

Allan Benton's timeless office, complete with a rotary phone.

reminders so sun-bleached one wonders why they remain. Doubtless the arrangement is part of a system practiced, polished and perfected over Benton's forty years in ham making, a career that's seen his products rise from obscurity to international acclaim.

THIS BUSINESS WAS STARTED IN 1947 BY A LOCAL DAIRY FARMER NAMED ALBERT HICKS, WHO RAN IT UNTIL 1973. At that time in his life, he was getting some age on him, and so he quit.

I was a struggling high school guidance counselor at the time, and when I saw the salary schedule for my profession, I knew right then that I had made a *poor* career choice. I thought, "Goodness gracious, I'll do this forever and not make enough to retire on." So, I resigned that day, though school had been open only for about a week. Right then, I told my principal that I just couldn't do it, that I could go across the street to the service station and pump gas and make as much money. I had to do something else, but I didn't know what.

A couple of weeks later, I heard Albert Hicks had quit the country ham business, and it got my attention. I guess I knew a fair bit about ham making since my family had always killed its own hogs, made its own sausage, bacon and ham—it was a way of life for us. But my grandparents took a lot of pride in the quality of their pork, and people always told them that they made the best ham and bacon.

So I asked Albert Hicks if he would lease me that old building and let me try my hand at making hams. And after some conversation, he agreed to it, and so I jumped right into it, operating on borrowed money the whole way. My dad mortgaged *everything* he had to get me into the country ham business. It's too bad that he died in 1995 and never got to see some of the attention our hams got.

I didn't know everything, so I started writing to every university in the South, even to European ham makers, to learn more about ham making. My goal was to make ham and bacon as good as any Europeans who were making it, which was ambitious, I admit. So with the help of a lot of people, I took what Albert Hicks told me plus what we had always done on the farm.

WE WERE SUBSISTENCE FARMERS, AND I GREW UP ABOUT TWENTY-FIVE MILES OVER THE TENNESSEE BORDER IN NORTH CAROLINA. I remember getting electricity and indoor plumbing! But that was an incredibly ideal situation for a hillbilly like me to grow up in because I learned so much.

I guess around 1978 or '79, I tried selling hams to east Tennessee tourist areas, such as Gatlinburg and Pigeon Forge. It wasn't going well at all. I was trying to sell twelve- to fifteen-month-old hams for the same price people were buying eighty-day-old hams. Back then, most of those cooks at restaurants didn't care a thing about quality. All they cared about was how cheaply they could sell their food.

I was literally starving to death trying to sell it. When I told my father I thought I was going to have to start quick-curing these hams in order to compete, he sat there a few minutes before he said, "Son, every time you play the other man's game, you will always lose. Make the absolute best that you know how, and quality will always win out." So I kept at it.

What started to change things for us was the farm-to-table movement. We really benefited from people starting to get serious about wanting quality hams and bacon.

My first white tablecloth restaurant was Blackberry Farm [a remote and exclusive resort in Walland, Tennessee]. If I could pinpoint my big break, it was that. Bob Carter was the chef there at the time, and later John Fleer came. It's a really nice place, and it hosts some of the best guest chefs in the country. They would see my products, and when they got back home, my phone started ringing.

The other key point for getting the word out was my attending the Southern Foodways Alliance event a long time ago [in Oxford, Mississippi] for a ham tasting. I was invited by [writer] John T. Edge to bring my hams there, and I literally thought that I would embarrass myself down there; I didn't want to go. Since it was in October, I thought I had an excuse since we're really busy, so I told him I couldn't come but that I'd donate the hams.

He wouldn't take no for an answer. He kept saying, "I want you to come." He kept telling me there will be lots of chefs and food writers down there who'd want to taste my products, and so I reluctantly said I would come.

What's ironic is my choice to take some eighteen- to twenty-month hams down there. My employees were saying, "You are surely to goodness not to take that old junk down there, are you?" They're like a lot of people who don't like older hams. But I said I was because to me, that's the way country hams are supposed to taste. When they kept saying, "Nobody will eat that," I said, "Well if they don't, then they can just go hungry because that's what I'm taking." And I took a bunch down there; I sliced forty-something pounds of prosciutto, which is a considerable amount.

Well, Sharon, my wife, and I went down there and fried a bunch of our ham, and throughout the whole event, chefs kept coming up to us and asking how they could buy some of it. So it worked out pretty well, I'd say.

On the long drive back from Oxford, Mississippi, to Madisonville, Tennessee, the whole time I was thinking that I was going to do a 180 in my business. I was making virtually nothing in the business—probably what a schoolteacher made! So I thought I'd take a chance.

I came to work on Monday morning—back when we only had three employees—and I told them, "I think there's a market for the aged hams we're doing for fine dining restaurants, and we're going to increase our production of those hams by 500 percent a year." I was probably doing one thousand hams that were eighteen to twenty months old, so that was a big increase. And of the fourteen thousand hams a year we do now, a lot of them are aged that long.

One of my employees, Albert—he's worked with me for forty years now—looked at me back then and said, "You are going to put us out of business." And I told him, "If we go out of business, then fine, because I want to go out in style. I want to make the best ham that I know how to make. I think there's a market if we can crack it."

Part of growing the business came from selling our hams to restaurants up north, and that wasn't easy. I'd call a chef in Washington, D.C., or New York or someplace up northeast, and I think they'd recognize a southern accent. Then before I could get ten words out, they'd say, "No, we're not interested.'"

So I thought, I'll just send them a ham, invite them to try it side by side with what they're using, and say, "If you're interested in this product, give us a call and we'll sell them to you." I probably only had to send out hams to about twenty-five restaurants.

NOT EVERYBODY UNDERSTANDS AGED COUNTRY HAM. One way to get them to is to ask if they know what prosciutto is. Of course, ours isn't exactly that because the Italians only use salt in prosciutto. We use salt, brown sugar and sodium nitrite in the cure, and we smoke our hams. But that's one way to get people to understand it.

Here's a good example of what I'm talking about. I was at an event in Baltimore where people were tasting different hams, and fourteen out of fifteen picked mine. When they asked the guy what he didn't like about mine, and he said it had too much flavor. Seriously! It had too much flavor! That was the best backhanded compliment I ever had!

WHAT'S FUNNY IS I DIDN'T KNOW MUCH OF ANYTHING ABOUT PROSCIUTTO FOR A LONG TIME AFTER I WAS CURING HAMS. When I first heard about prosciutto, I thought it must be some kind of a pasta dish. Literally, I'm telling you the truth! When I learned what prosciutto was, my kids were little. All three still in car seats. We were walking through a Fresh Market in Texas, and I was just looking at the meats. I saw a package labeled "p-r-o-s-c-i-u-t-t-o" and thought, "What in the heck is that?"

Customers from Florida talk with Benton (left) about why they stopped in at the store.

I asked the guy at the counter, "What is that?" And he replied something like, "Praah-chute-toe." And I thought, "I bet this is what they're all talking about." When I asked him for some, he asked whether I wanted imported or domestic? I asked him what each cost, and he said domestic was $13.99 a pound. Imported was $21.99 a pound!

Well, I told him I wanted domestic, of course, and I had him slice me a half pound because I only wanted a taste. But as he sliced it, I didn't really like the look of it because I thought it didn't have enough age on it. Anyway, I took it out to the car, ate some and handed some to my kids. And when they handed the paper back up to us in front, all the ham was gone. When I saw that, I took a U-turn in the parking lot and told Sharon I was going back in to get some of the imported ham.

When I came back out, they wanted to taste it, but I told them, "No, no more tastes. I want to compare this to my ham back home." Sharon said, "That's not the same thing," and I said, "Yes it is, only I believe my ham is better." So we brought it home, sliced some of ours really thin and tasted it, and she looked at me after a few moments of silence and said, "You're right, I believe yours is better."

HERE'S A GOOD STORY ABOUT SERRANO. I know some Spaniards who live in Florida and who would bring their motorhome here to get our ham. When they first started coming, they would stay out in that motorhome for about forty-five minutes in the parking lot, and I always wondered what they were doing. Well, what they were doing was whittling on that ham. And they came back inside and said, "This is the best serrano we have ever tasted." Well, I had no idea what serrano was, but they bought two or three more hams for themselves. And every time they would come back through here, they would buy several for themselves and for their neighbors in Miami. I had no idea what serrano was. That's how green I was.

But back to the prosciutto. I still didn't really know what I wanted to do with the prosciutto, but we knew we liked it and so we sliced it thin because the kids liked to snack on it. And when my eldest went off to college, I would make a half dozen packs of it thin sliced to take back to her dorm room. She told me, "Dad, people are flipping out over this prosciutto. You ought to sell it." I told her, "Well, Suzanne, I don't think there's a market for prosciutto," but she insisted. "I want you to promise me that you'll try it." She knew something I didn't.

So the next day, I sliced a bunch of it up and put it in four-ounce packages and put it out [in the store's refrigerated case]. And don't you know, we sold all of it! I never dreamed that there would be such demand. I had no idea there would be a market for it.

PART OF WHY I THINK OUR HAM TASTES AS GOOD AS IT DOES IS WE'RE WORKING TO GET THE RIGHT PORK. I pay more for it, but I like any of the old breeds. If I had to pick one, I might say Berkshire, or maybe a cross between two purebred pigs will be all right. And any of the old lard pigs [a hog whose weight ranges between three hundred and six hundred pounds] are all right by me. That intramuscular fat makes a wonderful country ham.

When I first started doing hams, not many were going after that kind of pork. I've got a guy now who's going to produce all Duroc hogs, and I'd like to get as many as two thousand hams a year from him. I want them kept on pasture and given no antibiotics. I want none of those hogs packed on top of each other like they do in these big hog operations.

Our cure is simple: salt, brown sugar, red pepper and sodium nitrite. Were it not for the USDA, I'd not use sodium nitrite because I still think my product is totally safe without it. They don't really force you to use it, but they virtually do.

I've been told that that unique flavor comes from that red pepper. [Benton describes this as a tanginess that, to my palate and nose, hints of ripe bleu cheese.] We use just a little pepper. We're not trying to burn anybody up. We're just following the recipe I grew up with, and I've just gravitated toward what we've always done.

Our fifteen-month ham really has that [tangy] flavor, but what's really interesting is it goes away when you age it to twenty months. Some like that fifteen-month flavor better than the twenty. Some days I really like the fifteen better, but not everyone does.

As Benton shows me around the facility, a customer greets him at the retail counter. "We've seen you on the television!" she says.

"You did? Well, let me ask you something," Benton says. "When's the last time you saw anything fit to watch on TV?"

"But you've got a reporter with you today," she says.

"No, this fella is writing a book on country ham, and he's interviewing the people in this industry I most respect," he says and turns back to our interview.

NOW, THE WAY I LIKE MY HAM BEST IS COUNTRY FRIED BUT NOT COOKED TO DEATH. Country ham, gravy and biscuits. If I'm taking a ham home with me, I want one with lots of fat on it. That's flavor. So when I'm cooking it, most of the time I'll add half a cup of brewed coffee to the pan after I've taken my ham off. I turn the heat to medium and let that reduce down to about what it was before I put the coffee in. My wife will do a cream-style gravy with flour and milk that's incredible.

IT'S NOT ALWAYS BEEN SO BUSY. I'VE HAD SOME TOUGH YEARS FINANCIALLY. If I'm around to make it another year, I call that a good year! Back then, I thought the future of the country ham business looked terribly bleak because people don't cook breakfast at home like they once did. I was worried that young folks wouldn't develop a taste for this kind of ham, but I was wrong. A lot of young folks like our product. But you know, most I know in the country ham business don't see a bright future in this. I do.

Part of our industry's challenge is not every customer understands country ham. They've heard of it, but they don't really know what it tastes like. And a country ham is a different type of critter from a honey baked ham. I've got a customer who's returning ten hams because she said they've gone bad. Well, you do have a bad one from time to time, but I've never had ten out of ten hams go bad, especially to one customer. I think she just doesn't understand what she's gotten.

ONCE I GOT SELLING TO RESTAURANTS…THAT CHANGED MY BUSINESS BECAUSE I BELIEVE CHEFS UNDERSTAND COUNTRY HAM. They also like having something that's a little bit exclusive. I owe a lot of my success to them, so I want to stay true to my goal of helping them have something different. Which restaurants do I sell to? I suppose a lot of them would like me to keep that private, so I will. I will say we sell to a lot of good restaurants in New York. A lot of our customers are on the Food Network—some of the best chefs in New York City, Charleston [South Carolina]. We also have a pretty good presence in Chicago now.

I really don't think every country ham has to be aged or handmade like we're doing it. [Industrial-scale producers] are doing a fine job. I might say that I think twenty months is the only good way, but others might like it aged just three months. They are a huge part of the country ham industry, and that's important. All the people my size are just a drop of water in the ocean of what they're doing. They're doing millions of hams each year, and we're doing about fourteen thousand.

Benton drifts back to shop's small retail area and is greeted by a customer. "I heard mention of you on TV last week when some lady was talking about Benton's bacon," she says.

"Oh, you did? That's really nice, but I'm just lucky they mention me at all."

"Well, you're lucky when you're good," she says. Walking toward the door, she adds, "I'm still waiting for someone to make an air freshener that smells like this room!"

I'd like to have someone take over the business someday, but not yet. We find people to work here, but we've had a lot of people come and go. If they don't buy into what we're doing, we let them go. I'm not looking for people who want a paycheck. I want them to care about what we're doing. I'm sixty-six, so I'm old enough to retire, but I'm not going to. …Albert's going to take my place when I retire. [Next to him is Albert, who's worked for Allan for forty years. "I'm seventy-eight and he's sixty-six, so I'm going to take his place when he gets old," Albert says.]

A while ago, Albert turned his notice in that he's quitting; it was a twenty-year notice. When I told him recently he's got eighteen years to go, he said it would take somebody that long to train them to do what he does. I'd say he's right about that.

Finchville Farms Country Ham
Finchville, Kentucky

Bill Robertson Sr. started Finchville Farms Country Ham for the same reasons many got into the business: a need of money. Working as the Finchville, Kentucky postmaster didn't pay enough to support his growing family, so he opened a general store out of which he ran his post office. He also cured hams for sale and built a solid reputation among Shelby County locals for a premium product. By 1947, the ham business was doing so well that he gave it his full attention.

Bill Robertson Jr., however, wasn't so fond of his daddy's ham business. When the school bus dropped him off each day, he was greeted with a lengthy list of chores to perform in the ham houses. After high school, he went to college mostly to escape the ham business, preferring summer work on an oil pipeline crew to shucking his father's in-bag cured hams.

It took the Korean War and a visit to that country by his father to change his thinking about Finchville Farms. Bill Sr. explained that the USDA was imposing new regulations on ham curing that would make their products safer yet add work to the operation. He told his son that if he joined him in the business, he'd do all he could to help him succeed.

After extended service with the air force, Bill Jr. saw the ham business anew. "I thought, 'You know, that doesn't look so bad after all,'" he recalled. Joining his father meant not finishing his last year of college, but at least he'd have steady income from a good business when he married and started a family.

Although the country ham business has changed dramatically since Bill Jr. got into it forty-four years ago, he's certain that it was his destiny. He led Finchville Farms to become Kentucky's largest country ham producer, and he helped create a 4-H country ham program that teaches kids the art of curing hams for entry into the Kentucky State Fair.

He sold the business to Tim Schweitzer in 2008, but the sixty-eight-year-old maintains his original office on the premises, visits daily and struggles to retire officially. As Schweitzer put it, "This is the man you need to talk to about country hams, not me."

MY DAD, BILL ROBERTSON, WAS A POSTMASTER WAY BACK, and he had a fledgling ham business. He could sell you a stamp right up here and could sell you a ham over back there. That's how it worked. I learned a lot from him, but even when he died in 1982, it was, "What the hell am I going to do with this?"

I WAS A SLAVE AS A KID GROWING UP IN THE HAM BUSINESS. When I got home from school, my dad would say, "We've got two or three jobs for you when you get over here." I heard that quite a lot back then, so I swore I was never going to be in the ham business if I could help it.

But in fairness to him, on Saturday night, he'd give you three dollars to go out on and loan you the family car, and if you burned twenty gallons of gasoline, he didn't say a word. Growing up and looking back on it, I'd say he was more than fair.

I was in college for three years and was in the Kentucky Air National Guard Unit that was activated in 1968, so I went to Korea. While I was over there, he came to visit me, and his big question to me was, "What are you going to do when this is over?"

I had a few options. I could go back to school, but to be honest, I wasn't the best student. It wasn't all that important to me. But I had a hell of a good time in Bowling Green [at Western Kentucky University]! My dad said that the federal government was going to require all small ham houses to comply with federal regulations, and if I would join him in the business, he'd do what was necessary to do that and help me. So I did.

This business has changed so much since I got in. It's like daylight and dark. In 1969, 80 percent of our business was whole hams. Now it's about 15 percent. That's happened because the lives of housewives have changed. What's today's housewife going to do with a whole ham? She'd have fifty-five dollars invested in that and have hardly any idea of what to do with it. She might not even have a pan big enough to put one in.

Family sizes are all smaller today. A small family can start eating on a whole ham prior to Christmas, eat it through Christmas, and then by the time February comes, they're dead tired of it. But that housewife today will buy a six-ounce package of biscuit cuts for just one meal because that's all she needs. I'm telling you, there will come a day when the whole ham will just be raw material for all the sliced products. It's not here now, but it's coming. I see it.

If we'd ever convince America to cook the country ham correctly, we'd never be able to meet demand. When you cook a slice, as soon as you see that fat turn clear, it's done. I like to grill it about thirty to forty-five seconds per side, and it's done. People think you have to cook pork to death. They don't know that country ham is certified trichina free, that it's safe to eat as non-cooked product. The real problem is we've eaten so damn much bland food in this country that when we eat something with flavor, it's like, "Wow!"

In this ham business, you have to think with two hats. Sometimes you think like a producer, and sometimes you think like a consumer. I need somebody to buy all that product, so I try to think like a consumer. But then I have to dream up a way to convince a man he needs a truckload of hams and think of how I'm going to put them on him!

Do we sell to white tablecloth restaurants? Yes, there's some of that, but it's limited consumption. I think it's a niche market. The few customers in that group that we have, they call the plant and UPS ships the ham to them. But we don't make any real contact with them.

What we do is called in-bag continuous cure. We apply the salt, sugar and peppers and then wrap it in two flat sheets of butcher paper. Then we slide it into a stocking and hang it. That way we don't have to re-salt. When it's in the stocking, it gets that football shape I like. No, it's not as much labor as you think, and those girls who do it now can do it really fast! At the end of the curing process, we shuck it.

Well, I learned this, I guess, by doing it. That takes a lot of time because this business is hands-on, all of it. When I'm in that ham house, I'm smelling the air, feeling the hams with my fingertips. I can walk into a room and feel the difference in relative humidity from one room to another. I can feel it on my arms, on my face. I'm not bragging; I have no idea how I developed that sense. Just over time, I guess.

When we get warm temperatures in the spring, those hams give up water and take on more salt. Then it takes summer heat to age hams, and when those enzymes are active—when temperatures get up around eighty—that brings on flavor. Mother Nature knows something mechanical refrigeration doesn't. We do an ambient cure, and that temperature fluctuation has some effect on it.

I really do think some of the drier years produce better hams. The flavor in some of those hams from the really dry summers was outstanding! Some of those hams would lose three-fourths of a pound each or more [beyond Finchville's target weight], but they were good. We like to keep our weight loss at 23 percent. Now, that extra weight loss hurts you financially, and you can't go to Kroger and tell them, "I've got to have more money because it didn't rain this year, and my hams lost weight." They'd say, "Are you crazy?"

I know nothing about hogs. I haven't been privileged to taste those [heritage-breed hogs] that people talk about. We buy all our fresh hams from a packer. People talk about those heritage breeds being the big thing, but these farmers will do exactly what the packers tell them.

I will say this: I've watched the hog industry change the pig dramatically in the last fifteen years. The good side is they've reduced the back fat on pigs. It used to be you'd get an inch and a half of back fat on every hog, but now that's down to five-eighths of an inch...and that's far enough. Now pork has become a dry meat because it's got too little fat. For years, packers saw 210 pounds as a big hog. Now packers are killing hogs are weighing 280 to 300 pounds. More meat, but still the same number of hams.

I sold this business to Tim [Schweitzer] in 2008, when I was sixty-three. I just couldn't keep up with the physical demands of it anymore. I made a wise decision to sell it, but I'm still here. Tim won't hear of me leaving for good. People have told me I've flunked retirement, but what else would I do?

If my wife came home and saw me sitting on her couch, she'd say, "Who's that stranger in there?"

I GUESS THE COUNTRY HAM INDUSTRY GAVE ME AN IDENTITY. I somehow felt that was a mark of accomplishment. I'm retired, but everywhere I go, people still ask me, "How's the ham business?" I like staying busy, I guess. I just love to be down there [at the business] on Sunday morning by myself. Some days, I'll go there for fifteen minutes, some days two hours—just putzing around. I don't hardly miss a day wandering in there. I've got to have a place to go every day. I get my mail there. My checkbook is still there, and I bet if you look around hard enough, you'll find the deed to my house there.

I HOPE MORE PEOPLE WILL TAKE AN INTEREST IN CURING HAMS. We've got a 4-H project in this state, something I worked very hard to get started. The first year we did it, we had forty-two kids from Mercer and Lincoln Counties, and [in 2013], statewide, we had more than seven hundred 4-H kids' hams at the [Kentucky] state fair.

Some of the kids get it, and some don't. It's the kids that show up the second year who are interested and want to learn what's going on, what it is they're really doing; 40 percent of their score is their ham, and 60 percent is an oral presentation. I've worked with a lot of them over the years, and to be there on the opening of the state fair and see seven hundred hams entered… well, that does an old man good.

S. Wallace Edwards & Sons
Surry, Virginia

In early December 2013, I called Sam Edwards III for an interview, expecting a rejection since Christmastime is absurdly busy in the country ham business. Yet surprisingly, Edwards was looking for a good excuse to take a breather; he took my call and even said, "Don't worry, no rush. It gives me a good excuse to sit for a minute. This is a whole lot more fun than being in that ham house. They can handle me being gone."

After almost forty-five minutes on the line, it was I, not Edwards, who had to stop the conversation. He's an energetic talker, smart, friendly and funny, the kind of interview that makes reporting a joy. He loves talking about the country ham industry—not shilling for it but rather naturally radiating his enthusiasm. Turning on Edwards's opinion spigot was easy; I dreaded having to turn it off.

Sam Wallace III gets some tutelage from his father, Sam Wallace Jr. *Courtesy of S. Wallace Edwards & Sons.*

Edwards's take on ham curing is linked inextricably to his family's time-honored techniques that convert ordinary eats into something sublime. Yet he is determined to see his hams, along with those of other respected American curers, earn the same regard lavished on the hams of Italy and Spain. Priced at around $300, his high-end Surryano ham is a steal compared to the $1,500 commonly required to purchase an Ibérico ham. Plus, Edwards believes that his ham is as good or better tasting. "People think, 'Oh, that's prosciutto, that's special.' And it is. But it's no better than what we're doing here. I'm proud of that. We all should be."

Speaking to the challenge of country ham making, Edwards launched into our conversation addressing what became 2013–14's crazy winter weather.

IT'S GOING TO BE EIGHTY DEGREES TOMORROW, AND IT'S DECEMBER 5! THAT MAKES US HAVE TO GO IN AND EARN OUR MONEY and pay attention because that weather is screwing with my Surryanos. It'll be cold enough soon enough, though. It always is.

We control our aging through managing humidity and airflow, and we use some air conditioning and heat. We know the humidity and the temperatures we want, and we let the hams follow the seasons' temperatures up and down. But we don't let it get too humid. That's the key to a lot of this. And if I lose some yield, I don't really mind as long as it's a better product.

It's a headache sometimes, but if you look at a globe, you recognize that we're in the perfect latitude where the best dry-cured meats are done. Get too far north or too far south, it doesn't work. It's just what we put up with because it's what makes all this happen. That's a good thing.

There is a certain amount of using your five senses in this to know if you're on the right track. Anybody can produce a ham that's safe to eat, but you'll ask, "Why does it not taste the same every year?" Aging hams is a whole lot like winemaking. A 2003 might not be as good as a 2009, and you never really know what you're going to get.

There is a certain time in the process when the ham is done as far as its flavor profile is concerned. Beyond that, all you're doing is drying the ham out, and that's all a little tricky. We don't want to harden the surface at the wrong time because the moisture *inside* can't get *outside* at an even rate. When that happens, the ham can spoil. So what you want to do is gradually pull the moisture out at a slow pace, no more than have to. You're fermenting the meat to the flavor profile you like by keeping all that in balance. Like I said, that's how we earn our money.

It's not easy to teach, fast anyway. It takes time. What you do to your product is hard to teach, to put into black and white, because you've got to see it. I take my kids and key players in the ham house, and rarely do I ever say what's wrong. I show them when it's right—the way they should look. I show them the positives and keep negatives out of the teaching pattern. If you're doing what's right, there won't be problems, but you have to be in there every day to know that.

I think a lot of the somewhat negative perception surrounding country ham was that it was born out of necessity. Nobody set out to make a culinary masterpiece like the Italians and Spaniards; they mostly were doing it to survive and have meat year round. Something so ordinary doesn't seem so exciting.

When I was younger in this business, I had chefs telling me we were missing the boat by not teaching more chefs how to use this ham uncooked. And what we've missed for too long was learning how good it is uncooked. But the problem is the USDA has created fear in everybody's mind about pork, that it *must* be cooked. So country ham guys are the beaten-down people in the meat industry because they're told they can't promote their product as ready to eat, yet it's perfectly safe.

What the USDA does is try to put us in a fresh meat category, which shows they do not understand a meat that is shelf stable. But as soon as you say it's like a prosciutto, they go, "Oh, okay! It's a pork hind leg, dry cured." Well, that's all country ham is, and it's worked safely for centuries!

It wasn't like that when my grandfather [S. Wallace Edwards] started this business [in 1926]. He was a ferryboat captain on the James River between Jamestown and Surry, Virginia. He grew up on the farm curing hams and made money selling ham sandwiches. He got out of the boat business and grew his pork business, added sausage and such.

My dad, Sam Jr., took it from little smokehouses in the backyard to more of a business and grew it further. Those smokehouses looked like wigwams, which is where our Wigwam ham name came from. So Dad was running it when the USDA got involved, and they about drove him crazy. He went from an independent business owner to a system in which you're being dictated to a lot. Dad told me my future in the business would be tough with all the government overreach, but since I grew up with it, it's mostly just part of doing business in the food world.

Well, I didn't know that I wanted to be in the ham business when I was younger. I was going to do great things on Wall Street, and I was the first in the family to be college educated. But when it came down to it, I either had to go to grad school to follow my original intentions or do the ham business. Before I knew it, I was up to my elbows in hams and started to like it. It's funny because I used to tell people, "Hell no, I don't want to be in the ham business!"

Restaurants have been good for us because they understand how to serve it uncooked. The Surryano [served in paper-thin slices] started as a kind of tongue-in-cheek joke made by a chef in New York. He took the name from us being from Surry and the ham being kind of a serrano style. I'm pretty sure Gramercy Tavern was the place and Tom Colicchio was the chef. He tasted it, said it was great and said to send him one. A month later, he had it on the menu, and the phone started ringing. People were asking for the Surryano, and we had to ask how they found out about it. When we realized we were getting a following for that ham, we trademarked the name.

In the 1990s, we were struggling with the flavor profile of our country hams because they'd become way too lean, not enough fat or marbling at all. Several years later, we came across Patrick Martins at Heritage Foods USA, which is in Brooklyn. He's helping sell [and distribute heritage-breed] hogs that are pasture-raised in the Midwest and raised certified humane. Lo and behold, the pork we got through him was better. We did blind taste tests on different breeds and cross-breeds and compared them with modern pork,

Aging hams at S. Wallace Edwards & Sons. *Courtesy of S. Wallace Edwards & Sons.*

and hands down, the better breeds came out on top. What I relearned was happy pigs make better-tasting pork because they're not stressed out.

WE'VE EXPERIMENTED WITH A LOT OF DIFFERENT THINGS, LIKE PEANUT-FED PIGS. In the old days here in Virginia, pigs were allowed to roam the peanut fields after harvest. But now they have very little waste in the harvest of peanuts, so you don't see them doing that. So now we're going back to using pasture-raised hogs like Berkshires, Tamworths and Red Wattles. My father used to say that pork is most like it tasted when he was growing up.

People want to compare our prices to commodity pork, but you can't compare it. It's too different. It's not what you get at the grocery store. Our Surryano is $350 at retail, but Spanish hams are $1,500 to $3,000 for a whole ham…and I'll slice mine against theirs anytime! Our Surryano is a minimum of eighteen months old, and 90 percent of

them are made from Berkshire hogs. Our problem is finding enough heritage-breed hogs because currently they're not raising enough of them.

THAT AGING PART IS TRICKY, ESPECIALLY WHEN YOU'RE DOING FIFTY THOUSAND HAMS A YEAR LIKE WE ARE. Mold's always an issue. Even good mold can get too plentiful. You don't want it to mat on the hams because it holds moisture to the surface of the ham. Mold used to be a benchmark: if you had the right color mold and the right thickness, it was a good country ham. It is good for flavor.

But most people don't [understand] mold, including the USDA. Some of these inspectors have never been in a country ham house, so we have to educate them. They'll see in their regulations that mold is bad, but I know the section in their regulations that refers to mold on dry-cured meats and know that it's not harmful. Just go into a serrano and prosciutto ham house in Spain or Italy, and their hams are covered with mold! But then they're cleaned, and it's taken care of. Same as ours.

Once I get to the flavor I like, I'll send the hams to cold storage, where they're refrigerated to twenty-eight degrees. One time, a place I sent my hams to raised the temperature of the cooler to forty [degrees Fahrenheit] to keep some produce safe. You should have seen the hams then! We had to scrub so much mold off them. But here's what's interesting: more people commented on how good they tasted and how they'd been really outstanding that year. I knew in my own mind, of course, it was because they'd be wrapped up in mold. When you get people who are only able to read a standards manual but not apply real science, you're going to get problems that shouldn't be. It's been done safely forever—*forever*—but not everybody gets that.

I DO WANT TO SEE THE COUNTRY HAM INDUSTRY MOVE MORE IN THE DIRECTION OF SELLING TO BETTER RESTAURANTS. That's instead of being the loss leaders in grocery stores that buy it from us for $1.20 a pound and sell it for $1.19. That does nothing for our image, but the way they're looked at by chefs now, that does.

It's kind of crazy to see them discover this food, taste it and say, "Wow! Where has this been?" when it's been around a long time. For us country ham guys, it's positive to experience that. No, country ham is not the new best thing, but it's great that it's being acknowledged. That's something my dad didn't get to experience, so I'm glad I stuck with it and have been able to see it come.

Broadbent's B&B Foods
Kuttawa, Kentucky

No country ham maker has won more Kentucky State Fair grand championships than Broadbent's B&B Foods, more commonly known as "Broadbent's Country Hams." The fourteenth and most recent time a ham from owners Ronnie and Beth Drennan won in 2010, it sold at a charity auction for $1.6 million (that's $99,688.47 per pound).

The Drennans didn't receive a penny of that loot, but the prize of priceless PR didn't hurt sales at all. Most importantly, it was further proof that the fifty-one-year-old business they bought from Smith Broadbent III fifteen years ago was in very good hands. (See sidebar for a brief history of the company's beginnings as told by Broadbent.)

Since buying the operation, the Drennans have grown sales by a factor of ten. Part of that boost came from a move to Kuttawa, Kentucky, where they built a modern, twenty-thousand-square-foot facility that produces twelve thousand hams per year. Their current trade is a far cry from their past businesses in gasoline distribution and as furniture makers. As ham makers, Ronnie and Beth have found their niche and are teaching ham curing to dozens of 4-H kids.

RONNIE DRENNAN: WHY DID WE GET IN THE HAM BUSINESS? OH, I DON'T KNOW. STUPIDITY, I GUESS. We'd had some other businesses prior to that, and this looked like a good change for us. We did pretty well with a gasoline distributorship and service station until the government began paying farmers not to grow crops. That meant we were selling a lot less diesel, and that nearly killed us. We never missed a payment on the business, but we never did as well after that. We sold it a while later.

Ronnie and Beth Drennan, owners of Broadbent's B&B Foods.

Ronnie Drennan inspects a rack of hams almost ready for smoking.

At the time we considered buying this business, we were in the furniture business. We made it and sold it through shops and such. A [business] broker we knew mentioned that Smith [Broadbent III] was selling the ham business, and though we didn't know much about curing hams other than my dad had done it, I got interested.

Beth Drennan: I guess the Lord knew what he was doing when he got Ronnie on fire to buy the ham business because it was the right move. About a year and a half after we bought the ham business, both of the businesses we sold went out of business.

Ronnie: When we bought the business, it was mail order and a gift shop. It didn't take long to understand we weren't going to make it in this business just on that alone. Mr. Broadbent told us we were going to have to grow it because he'd never promoted it in any way. He had his farm, he had motels, so basically the ham business was his hobby, his passion. His family didn't want anything to do with it.

Beth: He wanted somebody to buy it that he could mold. He wanted to teach his way to carry on that tradition. He really loves the fact we've grown it like we have.

Ronnie: Sales that first year were $200,000, which wasn't a whole lot. If all goes right, we'll get over $2 million this year. Smith did about 3,500 hams a year when we bought it, but we'll do about 12,000 now. We also cure some hams for other ham makers who don't have USDA-certified [curing] facilities. If you want to do mail order, you have to be certified. A lot of that [$2 million] is our bacon business, which has outgrown our ham business.

Today, we'll do more bacon in a month than we used to do in a whole year. Part of why it's so popular is there's not a lot of dry-cured bacon out there, though there's a lot who call it dry-cured. They might hang it a day or two, but they're not hand-rubbing it with salt and sugar like we're doing or smoking it like we do. There's a big difference in the taste.

Our facility is temperature controlled throughout so we can cure year round. We like to keep our hams in about an eight-month rotation. The people doing ambient cure are risking a lot depending on the weather. We'd rather not fool with that. It's easier if you control it.

I like to keep them in salt for twenty-eight days. That's the way my dad did it. We equalize them at about forty-five degrees, and when we start aging, we run the temperature up to somewhere between sixty-five to eighty degrees. They stay there for three weeks. Once it's out of equalization, it's lost about 18 percent of its weight, but once they're finally done, they'll lose about 25 to 30 percent. That's a lot of shrink.

We do smoke our hams, but I don't think it puts much flavor into them. I think it's mostly cosmetic, which is important, too. We use a smoke generator to blow cool smoke into the room where the hams are hanging. We don't want to put any heat to it, so it won't get more than 5 degrees warmer than the temperature is in the room. If it gets too warm in there, it sprays water into the smoke generator and cools it down.

Beth: Ronnie won't tell you this, but he's really good at trimming hams.

Ronnie: I think they look so much better.

Beth: Other people tell him he should have a workshop on trimming hams, and he says, "Come on down and I'll show you how to do it." I think that when we were doing furniture he got really good at details. He was picky then, and those same details make his hams look so neat.

Ronnie: I like my hams when they're around eight or nine months old. Not much more. We don't sell anything before six months.

Beth: If you're going to cook your ham, that's a good age for us old western Kentuckians. The older hams can be too dry for cooking. At this age, they're not too spongy, but they've gotten flavor from aging. We're old-fashioned. We eat our ham cooked.

Ronnie: People around here will say, "I don't want any of that old country ham." But when a New York travel writer comes here because we sell ham to a restaurant in New York—and they like it that way—that's fine. But people here won't eat it [uncooked].

Sure, we like hearing that it's appreciated in other places and that people pay good money for it. But it's not easy to sell it for more down here. People aren't used to paying a lot for country ham, and ours costs a little more than most. The small producers' problem is convincing customers that our product is worth paying the extra money, especially when we're in competition with the larger ham makers that don't charge as much.

I'm not going to knock Harper's or Clifty Farm or any bigger competitor. They've done a good job building their companies. We just do things differently.

Beth: But we hit that price competition head-on when we first started building our wholesale business and trying to get outside of this area. This business is tough for small companies.

Ronnie: It does concern me that this might be a dying art, at least on farms. It used to be that everyone had somebody in their family who cured country hams. But today, there's no farmers curing hams. There're less and less ham producers. You take Leslie Scott, Charlie Gatton and Smith Broadbent—they built their ham houses on their farms. Smith's ham house was right behind his house. It was one part of a lot of things they did.

It All Began with Smith Broadbent III...

As Smith Broadbent III tells it, his father, Smith Jr., and his father's friend Barry Bingham Jr. were duck hunting about a half century ago when Bingham proposed a business venture. Bingham—a Louisville media mogul whose family then owned the *Courier-Journal* newspaper, WHAS-11 TV and WHAS 840 AM radio—loved the country hams made by Smith Sr., who cured them just to give as gifts. Bingham believed that he could sell them and convinced Broadbent to make a business of it and let two of their sons run it.

The ham business began in 1963 as a partnership between Smith Broadbent III and Robert Worth Bingham III. Smith's identical twin brother, Robert, would raise and process the hogs; Smith III would cure hams in a production facility in Cadiz, Kentucky; and Bingham would manage sales and marketing in Louisville, where he lived.

Smith III, who held a master's degree in meat science, called on his former professors at the University of Kentucky to help him build a ham curing operation to meet evolving USDA regulations for mail-order sales. Although home country ham makers had sent hams elsewhere through the postal service for decades, regulations instituted back then mandated that any ham ordered by mail required federal approval for sanitary practices.

Broadbent and Bingham Food Products began curing hams in 1963, and in 1964, its first batch of aged hams was ready to sell. The business had a modest start, but sadly, in 1966, Worth Bingham died in an auto accident at age thirty-three, leaving Smith III to manage the ham operation alone. He bought Bingham's share of the business, renamed it Broadbent's B&B Food Products and closed the Louisville office.

"It never really got off the ground in Louisville," said Smith Broadbent III. With construction of the four-lane Western Kentucky and Pennyrile Parkways started but far from complete, Broadbent faced a minimum ten-hour round trip on two-lane roads to manage his Louisville interests. "I didn't want to travel that road two or three times a week, so we closed it."

Later, when a UK professor tasted one of Broadbent's hams, he convinced Smith to take it to the Kentucky State Fair's country ham contest. Eager to see how his ham would stand up to competitors', Broadbent entered and won grand champion. He would repeat that feat seven more times.

Wishing to sell more of his products, Broadbent believed that country ham needed higher market visibility. So he helped found the Kentucky Country Ham Producers Association in 1982. "I figured that if we all worked together, we could promote the product better," said Smith.

According Katie Broadbent, Smith's wife of fifty-four years, association numbers peaked at thirty-five producer members, but that's since declined to eight. "A lot of the people who were in business back when we started are out of it now," she said. "Some were bought out by others, but most just didn't stay in the business or didn't have anyone else to carry it on."

When Broadbent was diagnosed with prostate cancer in 1998, he had to end the juggling act of managing a large farm, a seed business and a country ham company. In reducing his responsibilities to focus on treatment, he chose "the farm operation because I liked it the best and because I didn't have a federal inspector there every day. ...It's as though they kept their jobs by finding something to write you up on every day."

Their daughter, Sarah Broadbent Rogers, who'd worked in the ham business for eight years, took over the operation briefly before telling her parents, "Please, sell that business!" "She was like Smith: she'd had enough of it because of that inspector. Sarah and her husband farmed, so she had enough to do with helping him."

Although Smith was approached by multiple buyers, none of their plans for his operation's future pleased him. Katie said that he fretted over finding the right buyer for an entire year before settling on the Drennans. "He was very picky because he wanted to make sure that whoever bought it was going to maintain it the way he had envisioned," she said. "Smith interviewed a lot of people before he was sold on Beth and Ronnie [in 1999]. They have been absolutely perfect for the job."

Both at age seventy-six, Katie and Smith still have businesses. He farms, and she runs Broadbent's Food and Gifts, an expansive shop in Cadiz, Kentucky, that includes a bridal registry. Neither has a plan to slow down. "We're doing what we like to do," said Smith, "so we'll keep on doing it."

So when the Kentucky ham producers came up with the idea to preserve this dying art, they wanted to get kids involved. When we started it about nine years ago, there were only forty kids statewide. In 2013, there were about seven hundred kids who cured hams for the state fair. Just at our place, we had kids from seven different counties who cured hams here.

Beth: The kids are a lot of fun to have here, and they really take pride in it. Watching them grow up, make their hams, do their speeches and get to hear what they've learned…that's great.

Ronnie: No, we don't have anybody in mind who'd come up and buy us out some day. We're pretty far away from retiring, so it's not something we think much about. You'd like to think one of these kids we teach might do it, but it takes a lot of know-how to run a business like this, a lot of time to learn it. We're still learning it. I can tell you that!

Father's Country Hams
Bremen, Kentucky

Charles Gatton Jr. didn't care much for his father's country ham business growing up, although he helped out when needed. After graduating college, he was a successful farm supplies salesman and store owner in Bremen, Kentucky, a tiny town located one hundred miles southwest of Louisville, Kentucky, and minutes from the Paradise Coal Company's mines and the Green River, which John Prine sang about in "Paradise."

As Charles Sr. grew too old for the physical work of ham making, "Charlie" found himself drawn back into the business, but not against his will. He liked customer service and preferred the time alone spent cooking and cutting hams before hustling off to his day job or overseeing their family's farm.

But most appealing was the urge to preserve the family's 173-year-old ham making heritage. In 2000, when his father died, Charlie made Father's Country Hams his sole focus. He's since expanded the business's line of gourmet bacon (one version is flavored with chocolate and another with vanilla and bourbon) and smoked sausage, plus a wide range of condiments and even dog treats.

I'M SIXTY-ONE YEARS OLD, AND BREMEN IS HOME. THE FARM HERE HAS BEEN IN OUR FAMILY SINCE 1840, WHEN MY GREAT-GREAT-GREAT-GRANDPARENTS

STARTED IT. They cured hams for themselves, but not as a business. It was their way of life. Even when I was a kid, you didn't much go to a store and get a country ham. Either you did your own or knew somebody who did. There's so much less of that now.

My father started curing hams as a business in 1959, when he'd been doing it around ten years. He really was a farmer with an interest in registered Hereford cattle, and he also was on the school board here—was its chairman for many years. He liked the ham business well enough to take it on full time, and he made great hams. When I started helping out, I was about twelve years old, but to be real truthful about it, I wasn't interested at all.

My father was a very outgoing person, friendly. When he was older, he loved to sit in his chair in the shop and talk to customers. That's my goal this year: to do more talking to customers. It gives people a sense of feeling for our products. It lets them know where this is coming from. It's part of who we are.

I USED TO SELL FEED FOR PURINA, AND I DID WELL AT IT. I was still involved with the farm and came back to the hams, but they were a sideline for me at that time. But as Dad got older, I got more involved. I was very successful with the farm supply business, and I enjoyed that. I won quite a few major awards in that business with Purina and liked what I was doing.

But after Dad passed away, and I got to looking at what I *should* be doing, it got more appealing. I knew any guy down the road could sell feed, but he couldn't do this. That meant something. It had been in our family for years, and I wanted to carry that on.

Marketing is a big part of the ham business. You've got to get exposure, so we did some trade shows. My wife and I went to the National Country Ham Show in Lancaster, Pennsylvania, in 2000, and we won the national country ham award. That put me back into the motion of doing what I really wanted to do. We did the Fancy Foods show in New York City, and we'd sell quite a bit of product through that. But when you factor in all the cost to do the show, we weren't making any money on going. We really wanted to carry on the Gatton heritage, but we were going to go broke if we didn't control our expenses!

WE'VE BEEN ON THE FOOD NETWORK A FEW TIMES; ONE TIME IT WAS ON A SHOW CALLED *CRAVE*. When Andrew Zimmern came to Louisville for his show [*Bizarre Foods America*, in 2013], he went to Morris' Deli for a country ham sandwich, which used our hams there. Boy, that was good for us! We've been selling them one hundred hams a month ever since. Being on the Home Shopping Network surely didn't hurt anything either. It was a good experience for us; it taught us a lot about how professional food stylists work, and it also helped build our customer base.

BUT STILL, I THINK IT STILL GOES BACK TO WORD OF MOUTH. PEOPLE MAKE THE SALES FOR US A LOT OF TIMES. Facebook is turning out to be that way for us. It's a growing thing, so we have to stay up with the times even though we're kind of old-fashioned. Now, 90 percent of our business is from the Internet and from corporate sales. We'll do some sales in the store at Christmastime, but not like we used to.

Country ham making is not a high-profit business. Part of that is because there's a limit to what you can charge, to what people will pay for bacon and ham. We've tried so hard to hold our prices down that we had to do something or quit. Our margins were so low we weren't making much money. Nancy Newsom [owner and ham maker at Col. Bill Newsom's Aged Kentucky Country Ham] tells me all the time to raise my prices. "I promise, Charlie, they'll pay for it," she says, and she's getting quite a bit more than I am. Maybe I should, but I don't know. Right now we charge around seventy dollars for a whole ham. It's not an inexpensive piece of meat.

PART OF WHY HAMS ARE EXPENSIVE TO MAKE IS THE LABOR. Every ham we make is moved twenty-six times, by hand, before it's sold. That's from salting to washing to drying to hanging and smoking, and maybe cooking or slicing. It's a 100 percent handmade product, and we're not going to change how we do that to compete with the mass-produced people. Fact is, we can't. For us to make just two dollars a ham like some of them do—you're better off to stay at the house. In fact, now bacon is what's keeping us in business. Demand for it is really strong. We've been featured in *GQ* and *Esquire* for our bacons.

It's tough for small producers like us to compete with bigger companies. We do three thousand hams at a time, but the big companies…some do a million every year. Since people like us and Scott [Hams], Newsom and others are little, suppliers don't always want to give us the hams we need when we need them. We buy in much smaller quantities than bigger producers, so it gets a little scary if you think you're not going to get quality product.

Big customers are hard, too. Restaurant customers of ours that seemed glamorous to have at the time weren't always very easy to work with. A famous restaurant in Tennessee—*that will remain unnamed*—wanted us to furnish them with $100,000 worth of inventory but not pay us until the Christmas holidays were over! We can't do that. We'd be in big accounts that would tell us, "We'll pay you when we can." Well, I got to the point that I decided I wanted a paycheck, and so we're not working with them anymore.

Hams hanging in the store at Father's Country Hams.

I don't know that I'd really call ham making hard work. When I compare it to bailing hay….no! That's hard work. I guess it seems like hard work when you're doing it, but it doesn't last long. We can cure eight hundred hams in three hours' time. That's taking them out, rubbing them in the cure and stacking them. That's not what I really consider hard work. But then again, I'm sixty-one years old. I don't go quite as fast as I used to.

Our hams are cured in a mixture of salt, brown sugar, white sugar and sodium nitrite. That last one keeps the USDA happy and allows us to ship. We keep them in the cure for about five weeks, and then we wash them off, hang them and air-dry them. We like to use natural ventilation when we can to help the flavor.

The younger generation likes our ham because it's not so salty, and that's due partly to our use of nitrites. When you use nitrites, you don't have to use that much salt to be sure the ham's safe. That often scares people away from country ham; they just think it's too salty. The problem is it's probably overcooked.

So, once the hams equalize at about fifty-five to sixty degrees, we smoke them to get the color we like. We build our fires in kettles outside the smokehouse and wheel them inside to work. Once they're fully aged—and our basic country hams are eight months old—they've shrunk by about a third. That's a lot of loss, but that's what develops that flavor. Our prosciutto-style hams are close to 34 percent shrink; they're aged ten months and hung at the top of our smokehouse to get that heat.

We haven't changed anything in our process since our family began making hams in the 1800s. We even have one of the last hams we cured when my dad was alive in 2000. We took it to the Fancy Foods show in 2006, put a birthday hat on it and a sign that said, "Kiss me, I'm 6!" It's in a cooler somewhere. No telling what it would taste like now.

I'm not sure what I'll do with the business when I stop. My son likes farming a lot more than this, so I'm not sure he's too interested. I'd like to think it would be one of my grandsons. What I know for sure is we'll never sell this business to anyone outside our family. Wouldn't allow someone else to use our name.

But right now, we have no desire to quit. Our equipment is paid for, and what else would you do with buildings like these? Not everybody needs a big smokehouse. For now, I'm still coming in at 5:30 in the morning, and I might be here cleaning until six to seven o'clock at night.

I enjoy cooking hams, and I can probably debone a ham in two minutes. It takes me two hours to do thirty-four hams—deboned and glazed. Those times are kind of nice because I'm in there by myself with the radio on and working, just doing my thing. I take pride in what I'm doing.

Harper's Country Hams
Clinton, Kentucky

Curtis Harper didn't have Facebook, Twitter or Instagram to advertise his fledgling country ham business in 1952. He had railroad workers who needed food that lasted unrefrigerated while they guided trains along the Illinois Central Railroad. A lifelong farmer, Harper started curing hams for the family larder and sharing them with friends, who became "hamvangelists" and spread the word about the mild, not-too-salty, lightly smoked hindquarters.

Demand grew quickly, leading Harper to stop raising hogs and buy hams from suppliers to keep pace. About two decades after opening, his operation had grown from a smokehouse made from an outhouse and salt boxes made from casket crates to a modern, fifty-thousand-square-foot operation curing 200,000 hams a year.

His own persona grew with equal vitality. Taking a cue from the Boss Hog character on the Dukes of Hazzard *TV show, Harper became "Boss Ham." Wearing a white suit, an oversize cowboy hat and a string tie, Harper wheeled his white convertible Cadillac through parades and nearby towns to promote his business by sharing samples. He was a natural in the role, happy to please fans and expand a business he envisioned would remain in his family for many generations.*

Tragically, Harper's life ended in 1995 when he was murdered in a predawn robbery of his store. An autopsy found that even at eighty, Curtis Harper was in fine physical and mental health. According to family members, he stayed busy creating new products right to the end.

His son, Gary Harper, and his wife, Dolores Harper, assumed the mantle of the business. When Gary died in 2007, Dolores and Gary's son, Brian Harper, took over and continue to run it as president and vice-president, respectively.

As one of the industry's largest players, the Harpers want to modernize the perception of country ham through marketing to younger generations. Giving out samples at large music festivals such as the annual Music City Eats in Nashville, the Harpers' country ham is awakening the palates of Gen Y and Gen X, young adults "who've never tasted country ham, but really like it when they do," said Brian Harper. "It's almost like a shock comes across their face, and then it becomes a real pleasant surprise. It kind of makes you realize how good it really is all over again."

BRIAN HARPER: COUNTRY HAM, I THINK, IS THE BEST-KEPT SECRET OUT THERE IN TERMS OF A REALLY UNIQUE EATING EXPERIENCE. Part of what's hurt it in the past is how people overcook it. People don't always understand that you don't have to cook it like you do a raw product like hamburger or chicken. To

Brian Harper, vice-president, Harper's Country Hams and grandson of founder Curtis Harper.

me, it's done when you start to get some aroma coming from it. Like I said, you don't need to cook it much at all.

I like to put it on a charcoal grill with maybe some hickory chips down under it. That's just amazing—it really is! People don't think about throwing a slice of ham onto the charcoal grill when they're doing hot dogs for the kids, but it's a great way to eat it.

Dolores Harper: I've been in this business since the '60s, after my husband got out of the military and we moved back here. We were stationed at Fort Hood [Texas], where they had no country ham. I grew up in Paducah [Kentucky], so I knew about country ham, though I didn't always like it. What I'd known was my grandfather's old-fashioned hams, which were too salty for me. But my father-in-law's weren't like that—not near as salty or dry.

My first position here was in the sales room—just out front at the counter—but I got much more involved. On Saturday mornings, I would come over with my father-in-law, and he would check the weights on his hams, and I'd write the weights down. I was very familiar with the whole business before I worked up to the office. The business was still small then, and we probably had only a handful of employees.

BRIAN: THERE ARE A LOT OF STORIES AS TO HOW IT GOT STARTED. Curtis, my grandfather, was a farmer, and like most farmers at that time, he had some livestock and cured the hams to eat way down the road in the summertime. He would give his friends some ham, and a lot of them worked on the railroad. He kind of developed a name for himself that way, with people traveling up and down the railroad sharing their lunches and sharing his ham. People would ask where they got the ham, and they'd say, "That's Harper's ham." And so finally he kept getting so many requests for it, he started the business. He just put a sign out here by the road: "Country Hams Sold Here." That was it. The road out front of here, [Highway] 51, runs from the Cairo [Illinois] bridge that crosses the Mississippi, through Clinton and on down to Memphis. It used to get a lot of traffic back in the beginning.

WHAT'S FUNNY IS HIS MINDSET ABOUT ALL OF IT AT THE BEGINNING. GROWING UP IN THE DEPRESSION, HE DIDN'T WANT TO SPEND ANY MONEY OR WASTE ANYTHING. So he went to a funeral home and got those old wooden crates they shipped caskets in, and they were perfect for salting down hams in.

His first smokehouse was an old two-seater outhouse. Indoor plumbing was just coming in, and somebody was getting rid of it. He cut a vent in the top of it, built his fires in there and smoked his hams—*in a two-seater outhouse*! Obviously that was prior to federal inspection.

I almost never remember a time that my granddad didn't have packages of country ham in his car. Everywhere he went, if somebody found out who he was, people would joke, "Why didn't you bring us some ham?" And since he always had ham in the car, he'd pull some out and give them a sample.

OH, HE WAS A CHARACTER. I THINK IT WAS IN THE LATE '70S OR EARLY '80S WHEN HE TOOK ON THE "BOSS HAM" PERSONA. Granddad eventually made TV commercials where he played Boss Ham. My dad would be a butcher character who was always running low on country ham, and Boss Ham would show up and restock him. He'd say, "Never fear, Boss Ham is here!" His old white suit and hat that he used as that character are in the Hickman County Museum on display.

You know, our slogan used to be "The Perfect End," but not everyone understood that a ham came from the hind end of a hog. So when some thought it sexually explicit, we changed it to "Hamtastic!"

My grandfather insisted that I do every job here if I intended to be part of management someday. So, I worked each job, taking out trash and scrubbing floors and salting hams. To be right there in the middle of it back then was neat, but it's tiring to do. You're lifting twenty-three-pound hams, either putting them way down in a vat or hanging them way up over your head, all day long. And even though we've gotten a few pieces of equipment that help with that, it's basically the same process it's always been.

With the company growing like it did, probably the hardest thing for him to adjust to was the fact that he couldn't control everything. When you grow to eighty employees, you've got to let go of some things and trust some people. He wanted to know every nut and bolt that we had here in the plant.

Dolores: He was almost a perfectionist. He would get up at 4:30 a.m. every morning, even before his alarm went off, which is pretty typical for anybody who raised livestock.

Brian: He was a very hard worker. This business was his life. Even when the business was successful and he had the opportunity later in life to travel or to have hobbies, this was it. It *was* his hobby. *This* was fun. Most people think it's a shame he didn't get out and do more before he died, but that wasn't how he saw it.

Dolores: Even the day he was murdered, he came out to the office.

Brian: He was robbed and beaten to death early one morning. It was 1995, and Harper's had won the grand champion ham that year at the Kentucky State Fair. There was a good bit of press coverage of the company and him, and we think that might have drawn some attention to him or the company. Well, the newspaper had run an article kind of describing his routine, how he would come out and open up every morning by himself before anyone else got there. We don't know if somebody picked up on that or maybe a former employee knew that.

So apparently, one day, he brought the cash box out to the front of the store, like he did every day, and it probably had between $1,500 and $2,000 in there. We think somebody followed him, that they'd probably been watching [his routine] before that and knew what he did. Well, they had a confrontation, apparently, and he was beaten to death and robbed. The crime never got solved.

My father took over, and he had a different management style—not better or worse, just different. Dad had a computer, and Curtis had pencil and paper, and he was good with them. When my dad talked with Granddad about investing in new technology of any kind, he had to explain to him how it was going to make money, how it was going to help us. He wasn't opposed to changes, but you had to bring him up to speed.

Our processes here haven't changed much over time. On the sales, reporting and tracking side, that's changed a lot with the way we're all in a global information database with our customers. But the process of making hams, not so much.

We did have a machine that was a water-jet portioner. Instead of cutting pieces by hand, you'd lay a slice of ham down, a laser would [scan] it and two water jet arms would come up, trim the fat and cut the portion to the maximum yield. It was kind of temperamental and it could break down, and while we tried it for three or four years, we just weren't quite big enough of a company to put the volume through it. So we went back about a year ago to doing all that by hand.

Some 20,000 hams in the salt at Harper's. The plant produces 200,000 hams per year.

Sliced hams ready to be trimmed and packaged for retail consumption.

We also have a [mechanical] massager. When you get fresh hams delivered, you want to make sure to get as much of the remaining blood out of the meat to reduce any chance for spoilage or an off odor [caused by blood pooling near the hip joint]. That all used to be done by hand, but we have a machine that does it mechanically, which helps a lot.

We cure year round here, so we can't do an ambient cure and rely on the seasons. Our volume is too large for that. What we do have are rooms that mimic the seasons. When the hams are salted, they're in the winter room, which is cold, of course. Then they move to the spring rooms [to warm to fifty degrees Fahrenheit and equalize]. We then move them to a summer room, where they age and shrink more, and then the last thing we do is smoke them. When it's all done, our hams are aged at least three months, but some go longer.

OUR CHAIN RESTAURANT BUSINESS IS PROBABLY THE BIGGEST SLICE OF OUR OVERALL PIE. I'd rather not share our customers' names with you in print—I'm sure you understand. We do lots of slices for platters and biscuit cuts, and we have a seafood chain customer that uses a lot of our ham trimmings just for their side dishes.

Chefs especially have been experimenting with it, mostly by adding it into other things, and that's helping exposure. They take a little bit of country ham and add into their recipes, which just makes the flavor explode. It used to be about the center-of-the-plate slab of ham you ate with breakfast, but that's changing.

Groceries don't want to fool with whole hams anymore. They want everything sliced and packaged. By weight, groceries used to be the biggest part of our business. It used to be that you could buy a whole ham in a grocery store, and they would slice it for free. But for employee safety, most probably don't have a knife more substantial than a box opener these days.

RIGHT NOW, IT IS IMPORTANT TO GET BETTER EXPOSURE TO A YOUNGER AUDIENCE. And, yeah, it's a challenge to get exposed to the corndog and chicken nugget generation.

Dolores: But it's surprising when we go to food shows and see how many children and young adults really like the product. They have never had a chance to even sample it because the parents think they aren't going to like it. But when they taste it, the children continue to come back.

Brian: If we can get a person to put our ham in their mouth and chew it up, we're going to get a good response almost universally. If we can get them to try it, they'll be sold on it.

Dolores: We're promoting it differently now. We're doing a lot more shows like Music City Eats and advertising in magazines we've never been in. We're looking to get readers of Paula Deen's magazine and others like that. It's changed so much since I've been in it.

Brian: We used to get a lot of traffic on the highway out front. People would stop and come to the store. But with the growth in interstates, there's so much less of it now. It used to be that if you were headed north or south of us, ours was pretty much the last place you could get a good country ham, so people headed in either direction would load up.

COLONEL SANDERS USED TO DO THAT. He'd have his driver take him down here, and he'd load up on hams to take back to Claudia Sander's [Dinner House, in Shelbyville, Kentucky]. He had a white Cadillac, too. Interesting man. That he would come down here for our hams…that said a lot.

Rice's Country Hams
Mount Juliet, Tennessee

Rice's Country Hams in Mount Juliet, Tennessee, operates out of a wood-sided store constructed in 1886. Back then, the road fronting it was a single dirt lane. Later it was paved, widened to two lanes and designated as Highway 70, for many years the nation's only East Coast–West Coast interstate. That meant that tourist traffic was nearly constant when Ed Rice Sr. bought the grocery store in 1933.

However, improvements in automotive comfort and fuel mileage over the 1940s meant that drivers stopped less at the store, leaving Rice searching for a novelty to draw them in. Since his country hams were popular with locals, he figured that tourists might also love them. He was right. By hanging cured hams from the store's front awning, he caught drivers' attention and, most importantly, their dollars. By the early 1950s, he was out of the grocery business and focused only on curing just hams and bacon.

Today, Highway 70 is a five-lane road linking Mount Juliet to Nashville about twenty minutes to the west, and the store's once-rural location is now shared by businesses of all sizes. The historic store hasn't changed, nor have the ham-making techniques perfected by Rice and handed down to his son, Ed Jr., who bought the business in 1977. Ed Jr. increased ham production substantially before selling it to Ginny and Scott Dabbs, his daughter and son-in-law, in 2003.

ED RICE JR.: MY DADDY USED TO SAY, "THE FASTER AUTOMOBILES RAN, THE SLOWER THE COUNTRY GROCERY STORE BUSINESS GOT." He'd had that business since 1933, when he bought it from my great uncle. He built a fine reputation as a ham maker.

Scott Dabbs: Ed Sr. got the business to where it was curing about eight hundred hams a year, but Junior and his wife, Ginny, grew it to about four thousand a year. We do a little more than five thousand now. I've worked in this business for twenty-two years, so I got to learn from Senior and Junior. I got a lot of good experience handed down. Junior says I'm the best curer of all of us since I learned from Senior and him along the way.

Ed: Scott worked fifteen years here before he took over. He knows what he's doing. Most of my career is like my golf game: in the rearview mirror. I'm seventy-five years old, so I don't care anything about unloading forty thousand pounds of meat and salting it down anymore!

I CAN TELL YOU HOW TO CURE A COUNTRY HAM, BUT YOU CAN'T DO IT. We don't try to keep any secrets. It just takes a lot of experience, a lot of being in that ham house every day just looking and touching and smelling. Things change from day to day, and after all this time, we go in there knowing what we're looking for. Every time you go into that ham house, you learn something new. You figure out when you need to move fans and humidifiers, why some hams are coming along and taking the cure and others aren't.

Sometimes you learn the hard way. We all do that, don't we? Here's my point: Once a man and his niece came out here to learn how to cure country hams. He bought about five hundred hams, and we salted them down with them. Later that year, I needed some aged hams, and I asked if he had any left. He took me to his cooler room, and inside were his hams—hung upside down! And there was no air circulation in there, which meant his hams didn't dry out. You could push your finger into them. He lost every one of them. That's a lot of money.

IT SOUNDS SIMPLE TO DO, BUT IT'S NOT, REALLY. There's definitely some risk to this business. When we buy a truckload of hams, there's no assurance whatsoever that they're going to taste like that and look like that a year later [he points to finished hams hanging on the store's wall]. Still, you do pretty much the same thing every year. We put our hams down in the salt about the first of January, and it'll be February before they come out. Then March is when the warmer weather comes in, and they'll take the smoke.

Scott: Something we do that I think is unique to Rice hams is [that] after we salt them, we stack them with the hocks interlocked this way [he demonstrates by crisscrossing his hands] and let them sit there for three and a half weeks. That gives them their nice round shape. Why that's important is it gives you a big, pretty center cut of ham, and contest judges absolutely like

After taking over his father's business in 1977, Ed Rice Jr. doubled its output.

that look, too [he gestures to the 2013 Tennessee State Fair grand champion country ham hanging from the store's ceiling].

Ideally, you want to sell a country ham when it's ten to twelve months old. It's still tender, not hard, though it's been through the summer sweat. It's at its peak flavor when it's lost 33 percent of its weight.

I KNOW PEOPLE SAY THEY LIKE THOSE OLDER HAMS, LIKE THEY DO IN EUROPE, BUT THAT'S NOT EVERYBODY. I don't think they mean the same thing as older people who say that. People used to say they wanted a two-year-old ham back in the days when people killed 550-pound hogs—extremely fat hogs whose hams took two years to cure.

Now hogs weigh 250 pounds, so you don't want to age it more than a year since it has much less fat. At modern hog operations, every sow has a chip in her ear, and they're monitored. If they're not producing lean pigs, they don't stay around. I've been in this business twenty-two years, and I've seen the change to an extremely lean meat. I'd absolutely call that an improvement. You need just a little bit of fat for flavor.

Ginny Dabbs: You'll have one in a million customers who says, "I want a fat ham." When my grandfather ran the store, he'd not even let anyone pay until he'd cut the ham and trimmed the fat off. That's what he thought was fair.

ED: I THINK THAT'S PART OF WHY WE'VE DONE SO WELL. WE LIKE MAKING CUSTOMERS HAPPY. WHICH REMINDS ME OF A GOOD STORY. One day, a little old lady told me she wanted two sacks of sausage—one hot, one mild. Well, all our sausage is mild, but that day I reached over in that cooler and got her a sack of sausage and said, "Ma'am, this is the hot." I then went to another cooler and reached in for another sack of sausage and said, "This is the mild." She paid and left. She got what she came for: I had a satisfied customer, and I knew she'd never know the difference because no one person eats hot *and* mild. I knew she got that other sack for somebody else.

But thirty minutes later, a phone call came for me, and it was that lady. I said, "Ma'am, don't tell me you got those sausages mixed up," and she said she did. And this is when I knew I could think on my feet; I had to because I'd lied to this lady and thought I'd got caught. So I wondered, "What am I going to do? I can't tell her I lied to her because she'd lose faith in her ham man." So I said, "Ma'am, where is your sausage?" and she said it was on the kitchen table. And I said, "The one on the right is the hot," and she said, "Thank you so much!" [Ginny rolls her eyes and grins at the tale.]

Ginny: It *is* telling the truth that we do this work for our customers. It's got to be a labor of love. If you don't love this—because there's nothing fun about what we do here—you're not going to last. It's hard work. But this is my life, and the people who come in here are always grateful. They say, "Thank you so much for doing this. It wouldn't be Christmas without coming here to get our ham." What we do, we do for our customers so they can walk in and say, "I haven't had anything like this since my grandmother died thirty years ago."

Yeah, I am tearing up, maybe because it's our tradition, too. We live in a world that is so money-dominant that it changes too many things. This is something we don't want to change. You look at the biggest ham makers, who do ninety-day, quick-cure mass production, and you know that's what most people think of when they think of country ham. We could build a facility and, based on our reputation, make all the money in the world. But if we did that, we couldn't do what we do: give that same quality and service. It's just not the same thing.

Ed: With our process, nothing happens fast. A while back, the Opryland Hotel wanted to serve more regional food, and their head chef then, Siegfried Eisenberger, bought every country ham on the market to taste for himself. When he tasted ours, he said nothing compared to the flavor in ours. But when he told me he wanted five hundred hams the next year, I told him it would take me two years to get that much to give him.

Although officially retired from the business, Ed Rice still welcomes customers when at the store.

SCOTT: YOU'RE TALKING ABOUT CUSTOMERS...HERE'S SOMETHING YOU'LL LIKE: a letter from [actress] Dinah Shore that was sent in 1969. She wanted [Ed Sr.] to send a ham to [then actor and eventual U.S. president] Ronald Reagan. [Scott unfolds the weathered letter and points.] I found it in the shed out there, so apparently we thought a whole lot of it. Look here... somebody did some math on it. I guess they needed to add something up and saw a piece of paper on the desk. It's still kind of cool.

Ed: My daughter's right; this is hard work, with lots of long work after hours. My wife and I did it for eight years while I was still working at Ford Motor Company in Nashville. I'd take the Saturday before Thanksgiving off, start vacation and then take a leave of absence to get through the holiday season. And on Christmas Day, when the shop was closed, I'd start back to work at Ford. I did that for eight years.

I'VE BEEN ON TELEVISION FIFTY-NINE TIMES, BUT ONE OF MY FAVORITES WAS FOR THE MARTHA STEWART SHOW THIRTEEN YEARS AGO. I get a call from the producer, who introduces herself on the phone and says, "I'll be producing your segment for Martha Stewart, if that's all right with you." And I said, "Well, if it's all right with Martha, then it's all right with me." Then she asked me, "Where does a ham come from?" and I

The Rice's 2013 Tennessee State Fair grand champion ham hangs in the country store.

said, "From the south end of a northbound pig: the *arse*." I didn't get much of a reaction.

Later she tells me, "I'm a vegetarian." And all I could think to say was, "Well, most of us down here are Presbyterians, and you're going to be out of place with all these Presbyterians and pigs." I could tell we were going to have some fun with them.

So when they finally came, it was a big deal: fourteen people on the crew, and they filmed all day. That producer went into that ham house at that stage when the hams were drying, and she was holding her nose.

Scott: When they're trying to dry out, well, it's a distinct smell…kind of funky. It's not for everybody.

Ed: But they were all good sports about all of it. They later told us their field trip here was one of the most enjoyable segments they've done because of my humor. We fed all fourteen of them lunch in our home that day. Since they were from up north, we really wanted to show them some real southern hospitality.

Scott Hams
Greenville, Kentucky

Scott Hams, owned and operated by Leslie and June Scott, is one of the country ham industry's smaller producers (four thousand hams annually), but its lengthy list of awards includes an impressive sixteen national titles and two Kentucky State Fair grand champion wins. Its county's 4-H chapter, which makes its hams under Leslie Scott's guidance, has dominated the state fair youth category for more than two decades.

The Scotts met at Western Kentucky University and married at age twenty a half century ago, and they have cured hams for nearly fifty years while running a six-hundred-acre Angus beef cattle farm. The two seventy-one-year-olds say that they've never worked a day in their lives and that they enjoy working harder and longer hours than those a third their age.

They're also natural storytellers who seem surprised (but then pleased) when you laugh at their tales. Because their lives are so rich with humor—things that might not be funny to country folk but are gut busting to city folk—I've included several here that aren't necessarily "ham centric" but are too funny to leave out. I visited them in the early fall, when holiday ham selling season was just about to begin.

June Scott: If this was Christmastime, I couldn't talk to you like this. We'd have so much going on because we do half of our business in December.

We started selling hams in 1965, but we've shipped since 1969. Back then, you just took the hams to the post office in a cloth bag, fastened them with a wire and a tag and they'd go through the mail like that…I'd not say the Internet makes our business easier, but it's good for business.

Leslie Scott: I remember when my granddaddy shipped a calf through the mail to Bourbon Stock Yards in Louisville. Just put a tag on his neck and took him to the mail car and that was it. Never a problem. I never did that, but we do have beef cattle. High-end Angus. We have six hundred acres we farm, and I'm the guy who does that. I had major surgery on my back last

June and Leslie Scott, owners of Scott Hams.

year; they put in two rods along my back. I'm real lucky I can walk, but I'd have to say the farming's harder than making hams.

We got into hams when we did because we just thought there was a market in it. But we never worked at it like others, never grew it like some others. Harper's probably has ten salespeople. June's our only one.

June: I guess we've never been as ambitious as others. Maybe we don't know how to sell to other markets. We've done what we've always done, what our families did.

Leslie: We were good-size farmers in the 1970s, row croppers, and we had the ham business. I worked for June here for two or three years, and then Daddy sold me his farm, and so I pretty much let her do the hams. I found out, though, that June wanted that farm so she could get me out of here!

June [grinning]: Really, I wanted the farm to stay in the family. I said, "Les, you know we have to buy that farm, and you know we will. It's been my home since I was twenty." It was the emotional part. I couldn't see it owned by others.

But I know you want to talk about our hams, not that other stuff. …We'd always done country ham on the farm—my parents and his parents, too. And I guess we did them pretty well because people started asking if we'd sell them. We knew it was becoming a dying art, so we got in. We started with one hundred, and we sold those right off.

Leslie: When we started, the advice we got from our parents, though, was to not tell anyone you've got hams because they'll steal them. A long time ago, in the Depression, they'd say some people would go look in the windows at church, see who was there and then go steal their chickens. You'd get a dollar for an old hen back then, and that would buy a pair of overalls for ninety cents.

We started out with a little wooden building, which we put on a sled and pulled over to a tenement house where we lived. Granddaddy came by and opened the door when I was salting them, and he said, "You're going to lose every one of those hams!" His were in boxes, and ours were on a shelf. Well, it worked out fine.

In curing ham, you're trying to beat bacteria to the bone. The one that gets there first is the winner. If salt gets there first, you've got a ham. If bacteria gets there first, you've got a spoiled ham.

Our cure is just salt and sugar. No nitrites; our parents didn't use them, so we didn't. Nitrites make things real bright red instead of brown, which is the color we want.

June: And we smoke ours. I think it makes a pretty ham.

Leslie: Daddy swore he could tell the difference between a smoked ham and an unsmoked. So we gave him some of each to taste without telling him which was which, and he couldn't tell the difference. But smoked hams, oh, they smell good when you walk by. We build our fires for smoking out of hickory sawdust and sassafras. Sassafras is just our touch, a small difference.

When my daddy cured hams, he just used salt, but we added some sugar. We think it keeps the hams softer and makes them a little bit sweeter. Daddy wound up using some sugar, too.

June: Our customer base is pretty diverse, and a lot of it's come from word of mouth. A lot of the people who buy them are people who've not been in the U.S. too long. Foreigners. People who ate aged ham where they came from. Those are interesting stories.

There was a fella from here who was working for a guy in Chicago. He knew we had country hams, and he knew a fella who called me to ask if we had anything over a year old. I said, "Yeah, but you don't want it. It's hard!" That's never been my favorite type of ham. But he said to send it, and he liked it and wanted more. So I started choosing small ones that I put back to satisfy this man. I was selling them at the same price as these others, but I probably should have charged more since they shrink so much.

Anyway, so the guy in Chicago had a wedding, and a fella from Las Vegas was there. He loved the ham and called us and ordered six. He said, "I'll have a lot more customers for you," and sure enough, he did. Now we have a lot of customers in Las Vegas, typically foreigners who know what an aged ham is supposed to taste like. When they call, I'm the only one who talks to them and can understand them. They have no clue what Leslie's saying, do they, Leslie? [He grins sheepishly.]

So this fella from Las Vegas knew someone from Oregon, and he told him about our hams. And now we have a lot of customers there now. We also have some restaurants in California that use them. They like the ones that are a couple of years old and have mold all over them.

I suppose we could have sold more to restaurants since that seems to be popular now. But maybe we really don't know how. Still, we've been lucky. We enjoy this. We've been happy to make a living at it. I'd rather work than do anything. I'd even say I've never worked, really, because I love it.

I had a job in town when I first married Les. Then we decided I'd quit so we could start a family. But I'd have worked even if they didn't pay me because I liked it so much. Our pastor—who's gone now—once said, "When we get to heaven, we'll not have to work anymore." And I thought to myself, "Well, if heaven's like that…I don't know if I'll enjoy it much if there's not much work up there." Could you imagine going up there and not having anything to do?

But for me, it's the customers I like the most. That's fun. When they enjoy what you do, it makes you happy. Les, I think he likes the kids most, the 4-H kids he teaches to make hams for the [Kentucky] state fair. Those kids fall in love with Les, and he loves working with them, showing them how people survived a long time ago by curing meat.

Leslie: To me, that's more important than selling a ham to somebody in Las Vegas. When those kids start, they tag their name on that ham and stay with it through the whole process. And when they get ready to eat it, they can say, "I cured that ham." Our kids have won grand champion at the state fair almost every year we've done it. And they win nearly every category, too.

I'm more proud of that plaque right there than any plaque we've gotten. [It reads, "4-H Volunteer Hall of Fame. The Innovative, Creative and Enthusiastic Award presented to Leslie Scott, Feb. 2012."] That's because of the work I do with 4-H kids. It's fulfilling work for me. To see those kids wherever you go around here and have them ask, "How's my ham doing? Is it going to win this year?" We've won a fair share of contests, too, but it took some time.

June: Our meat inspector encouraged us to go to the National Cured Meat convention in Louisville and enter their competition in 1987. Well, it didn't turn out so well. We weren't last, but we weren't far from it, and we weren't very happy. But no one knew we weren't happy because we never said anything about it. We listened and learned.

Leslie: The next year, they had that convention out to Albuquerque, New Mexico, and since we couldn't afford a plane ticket, we set out to drive there. We put two hams in the back of the car and drove. We won grand champion that year and every year after that. Well, twice we won reserve [first place].

June: The year we won grand champion at the Kentucky State Fair in 2009 and our ham was auctioned off for $1.3 million, that's a pretty good story.

Leslie: The bidding almost quit at $40,000.

June: You have to know that the glass is always half empty with Les [she rolls her eyes]. We'd won that year, so we were at the head table at the [Kentucky Farm Bureau Country Ham Breakfast], and Les was saying, "It won't bring anything. The economy's down." So the auction starts, and it does stop at 40, and he said, "Well, that's it." But then it started again and started going so fast I thought I was going to have to sit in Leslie's lap to keep him in his chair. We'd never have thought the bidding would go to $1.3 million. [The highest-ever Kentucky State Fair auction price was $1.6 million, paid for a Broadbent's ham in 2010.]

Leslie: Yes, I was surprised.

June: The money all goes to charity, and the bidders get the ham. [Ham makers] don't receive money for it, but it's good for business to say yours was grand champion and it auctioned for that kind of money.

Leslie: I don't know what we'll do with this business when it's time to quit. I guess we're getting up there in years, so we need to consider it. We've had some people interested, but we've not made a decision.

June: It's not a decision we want to make until we have to make it.

Leslie: When we do, we want it to go to someone who will do it the right way, which is important and which is why I teach those kids. One day, I said to those 4-H kids, "I'm not teaching you to cure hams out of the goodness of my heart. I'm doing this so one of you can buy my business one day." Right then, a ten-year-old boy said, "I want to buy you out!" He wasn't quite ready, but maybe someday.

The Hamery
Murfreesboro, Tennessee

Few businesses spaces are as small as The Hamery in Murfreesboro, Tennessee, forty-five minutes southeast of Nashville. About 2,500 hams dangle from drying frames in neat rows seemingly everywhere on both floors of the 3,200-square-foot building, which was a veterinary hospital in the 1950s. Heavy black plastic sheets cordon off hams by age and style on the upper floor; in the basement, hams are crowded into coolers and rooms that radiate like spokes from a central production hub where they're cooked, cut and packaged. Owner Bob Woods's space-utilization savvy would impress the most cramped Manhattan shopkeeper, and the entire operation is neat as a pin.

Despite a lush mane of snow-white hair, Woods, at sixty-two, is a wise-cracking young-at-heart artisan who believes that at least part of his business's future is in country ham sales to high-end restaurants. The lawyer turned farmer turned ham maker moves easily throughout the tight quarters, pulling back black sheets to reveal "experimental" hams he wants to sell to "chefs who get what we're trying to do." That means culinarians who

Bob Woods, owner of The Hamery, maximizes every inch of his small building's space for ham aging.

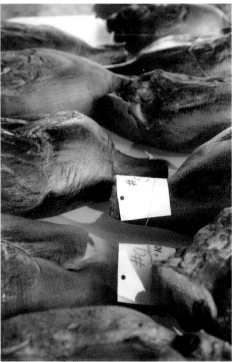

Top: Nancy Newsom, owner, Col. Bill Newsom's Aged Kentucky Country Hams.

Left: Country hams cured by locals for the 2013 Trigg County Country Ham Festival.

Above: The crowd fills Main Street at a ham festival.

Left: Newsom's Old Mill Store in Princeton, Kentucky. Many things are sold here, but you come for the ham.

Mold is gold on an aged ham. This ham is two years old.

Allan Benton, owner, Benton's Smoky Mountain Country Hams.

The very rustic retail rack at Benton's store. Expect no frills here, just amazing cured pork.

Paper-thin slices of Benton's fifteen- and twenty-month-old hams.

Left: Bill Robertson Jr., former owner, Finchville Farms Country Hams.

Below: Fewer customers want whole hams, making boneless packaged hams a hot item, Robertson says.

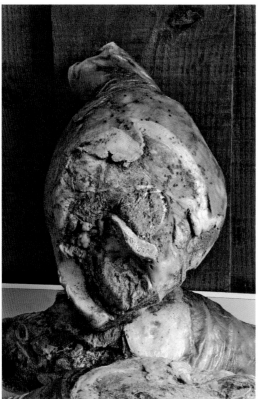

Above: Behind Robertson are the contents of one of four Finchville ham houses. When full, they can hold forty thousand in-bag cured hams.

Left: The finished Finchville product. This ham is used by chefs such as the venerable David Chang of New York City's Momofuku restaurant group.

These in-bag cured hams are ambient- or "weather"-cured hams. Robertson likes the unpredictable flavors yielded by weather changes.

The elegant and incredibly flavorful Surryano ham. *Courtesy of S. Wallace Edwards.*

Sam Edwards III. *Courtesy of S. Wallace Edwards.*

Broadbent's uses its ample space to cure hams for companies lacking some space. These are for Rice's Country Hams.

Above: Katie and Smith Broadbent III, founders, Broadbent's B&B Foods.

Left: Charlie Gatton Jr., owner, Father's Country Hams.

Above: Curtis Harper, founder, Harper's Country Hams, in his "Boss Ham" costume. *Courtesy of Harper's Country Hams.*

Left: Curtis "Boss Ham" Harper promoting his products. *Courtesy of Harper's Country Hams.*

Ed Rice, founder, Rice's Country Hams. *Courtesy of Rice's Country Hams.*

In the ham house with Leslie Scott.

Bob Woods believes that the key to the country ham reaching new customers is through long-aged hams served charcuterie style.

The curing season begins at The Hamery with the first salt application. *Courtesy of The Hamery.*

Mountain Ham slices are streaked maroon and ivory with meat and fat.

When carefully trimmed by Denham, a Mountain Ham yields a broad array of cuts. *Courtesy of Woodlands Pork.*

Curer Jay Denham covers the butt faces of Mountain Hams with a mix of vegetable oil and rice flour to help the meat maintain moisture.

Dan Murphey, president, Clifty Farm Country Meats.

Top: Tyler Brown, executive chef, The Capitol Grille, Nashville, Tennessee. *Courtesy of The Capitol Grille.*

Left: Robin Song, executive chef, Hog & Rocks, San Francisco. *Photo by Nader Khouri.*

Left: Michael Paley, executive chef, Metropole, Cincinnati, Ohio.

Below: Bob Hancock pets his Red Wattle breeding boar while feeding it scraps from his bakery.

happily pay $150 for just one hindquarter because they'll slice it paper thin for multiple dishes and net tidy profits for their restaurants.

But producing aged hams—many of his are up to two years old—takes lots of cash and the determination to wait. Woods acknowledges that the gamble for a business his size isn't small. Forking over tens of thousands of dollars for raw flesh that takes months to become edible and won't return a penny for almost two years unnerves most business owners.

"I know guys in our business who see the promise of a quicker turnaround, and you can't blame them for wanting their cash sooner," says Woods. "But that's not what we're doing. We're committing to a truly unique product."

This was my grandfather's veterinary hospital, here in the basement. And over here on this platform was a bunch of dog kennels. As a kid, I remember him having cows in the basement. Horses and cows would die in here, and they'd have to tie a rope to them and pull them out through that door. *Seriously*, I'm not kidding.

I'd always liked country ham, but I don't guess I ever thought about it being a business for me. I went to law school, but after I left, I knew I didn't want to do a desk and book job. My grandparents had a farm near Murfreesboro, and I wanted to do that, so I took over their place, row-cropping and taking care of about fifty heifers for about, I don't know, ten or fifteen years. I really liked it.

Then my uncle, Sam Woods, he and Tom Givan were doing the ham business, and they wanted to retire. So I thought it would be great to do that in the wintertime and keep farming in the summer. So I bought it in 1981. Sometime after that, my grandparents died, and the farm was split up [among family members]. I got involved in the ham business full time, and I'm still here.

I really like what I do, and I'd like to apprentice someone someday. I know I can't go on forever. But it's a tough business for a young person to get because it takes so much upfront capital. Just think about spending $40,000 to $50,000 in a year's time on some hams and then letting them sit there for a year or two with no return.

I see a guy at the [Tennessee] state fair every year who makes good hams. And I asked him, "Why don't you cure more hams?" He said, "I can cure just a few hams, grind the rest of it up for sausage and sell it tomorrow, or I can cure the ham, let it lose a third of its weight and then sell it for three dollars a pound next year." It doesn't make a lot of sense when you think about that way, now does it?

But I think where the ham business could go is to customers who want that longer-aged product. It's been popular for centuries in Europe,

Woods coats the butt face of his long-aged hams with lard to help them retain moisture.

so why not here? It's getting that way, but slowly. I went to the Fancy Food Show in San Francisco one time, and I saw all these long tables of hams from Spain and Italy. I have to tell you, those were fine hams, but I thought none of them tasted any better than mine.

And the prices they were asking! Of course, they don't charge as much in European countries; some of that's the cost of importing. But they're still expensive. I guess part of why they pay more there is their hillbillies have had much longer than our hillbillies to make and sell really good ham. They've already educated their customers on what great ham tastes like. We're only now doing it.

So A COUPLE OF SUMMERS AGO, I SET ASIDE THREE HUNDRED HAMS SPECIFICALLY TO AGE LONGER, AND I SET OUT TO VISIT SOME RESTAURANTS AND SELL THEM. It's really fun to go to a restaurant like Husk [the acclaimed Nashville restaurant owned by chef Sean Brock] and say, "You should try my ham." Husk was still under construction when I visited a couple years back, so [then chef Morgan McGlone] leaned it onto a sawhorse, cut off some ham and tasted it. They wanted it! When people try it, they're generally amazed.

Dave Cuomo, the pizza maker at Bella Nashville, called and said he wanted to come down and see what I had. He just showed up because he's that interested in his ingredients. It's just a little wood-fired pizza place in the Nashville Farmers' Market, but he uses a lot of our Tennshootoe ham. He's close to one of my top customers.

Eric Rubin, the [former] chef at Hog & Rocks [restaurant in San Francisco] came here and tasted our ham. He liked it so much that he wanted one to put in his backpack to take on the plane with him, but it wouldn't fit all the way. So I had to saw the hock off for him to fit it in there. Imagine the security guy at the airport seeing that big hog's leg sticking out of there!

I know he's taking my $150 ham, slicing it and putting it on a plate and selling it for closer to $700, which is a pretty good markup. But that's what you're seeing now, and I'm working to target more people like that. To find people in this industry who are super-talented and appreciate my product like that, I feel it's the greatest achievement.

As exciting as all that is, realistically I don't have a grasp yet of the kind of attention our ham's getting. Our business still comes mostly from people who want to cook a whole ham for the holidays or have it sliced for biscuits or breakfast. It's not the people with the gourmet palates who want it…yet anyway. For thirty years, I've been trying to keep moisture in my hams because everybody cooks it. But now part of the market wants dry hams they can slice.

Part of that older mindset, I think, is the history of the South. For many years, this was an agrarian society that used their hams to feed themselves. They couldn't go back out to the field with a little bitty slice of charcuterie. They wanted a thick piece of meat, and they probably put it on biscuits made with lard. They needed sustenance, a lot of energy to help them work. They didn't cut that ham thin like they do in restaurants now.

So, trying to serve a new market puts me in a bad spot sometimes. I've got a block of two-year-old hams, and another block I want to set aside for next year to age. Logistically, I've got to think two years out. But you've got people coming in who want to get a ham for Christmas *now*, and I have to tell them I'm out even though I've got them back there. You piss some people off sometimes.

I'm not convinced these heritage-breed hogs are what everybody wants for hams. Some of your restaurants want them. I've got a couple here I'll show you. [He produces a pair of hams in salt from a Berkshire pig, their hooves still attached, from a box inside his walk-in cooler.] I told the guy I got them from that I'll salt some down and cure them out to see if there's any difference from what I'm already using. I really do want to learn, but I'm not convinced I need to pay four times what I pay for the ham that I get now and then try to get that money back out of my customers. Customers rule the game, so for me to mark my hams up that much without any difference in taste. …I'm not convinced yet that it's worth it.

I'm also not convinced consumers want that much fat. Whatever the consumer wants, he'll get. See those hams over there? They have a little more fat than we're supposed to have. Most customers don't want that big slab of ham with that much fat on it. We bone ours, take the skin off and vacuum-seal it. The only work for the customer is to choose what they want to do with it: slice it, bake it whole, whatever.

Ham making isn't rocket science, but it's just not that easy. I used to have a humidity meter in here, but I never paid much attention to it. I knew that if mold started developing on the hams, I needed to bring in the dehumidifier. If rain is coming, I turn the dehumidifier on to get ahead of it. But even if I didn't use those, I could still cure hams. What's great about the upper South is the climate is perfect for this. It gets cold enough to slaughter hogs in the winter, salt their hams and age them out properly to develop those flavors as it gets hotter.

I use salt and sugar only. No nitrites. I do it that way because I was told to do it. Sugar cuts the harshness of salt, and I also think that on the two-year hams, you're getting some mellow sweetness from it. It's getting a buttery texture.

When the hams come in, we just get some salt on them and get them in the cooler as fast as we can. After that, we salt them two more times, rub it onto the hock like that and over the top like it were snow covered, just to where you can't see the meat. I go back two more times to add more salt because I've found that they can get dry on the surface. And if the surface of that ham dries out, it won't take the salt. If it stays moist, it'll continue to take salt.

Overall, they're in the salt five to six weeks. About the middle of February, downstairs in the basement, the temperature is perfect, about fifty degrees, and it stays there until late spring. That's where they equalize for three weeks. After that, we smoke with hickory and apple woods and age them out.

These are some 2012 hams, ones I call Tennshootoe. [He points to a batch of long-aged hams named to echo "prosciutto," but with a Tennessee twist.] You like that name? I thought it was kind of clever. We put lard on this part to keep them soft. [He points to the butt face, the area where the leg was cut away from the hog's carcass, which is smeared with lard to form a natural protective covering.] The Spanish do their serrano hams like this.

We remove the aitch bone, which generally most prosciutto ham makers do because you can have problems around bones. [The aitch bone, one half of a hog's hip joint, is a highly vascular area that can harbor trace amounts of post-slaughter blood. If not reached by the cure, it can produce unappealing flavors and aromas in that area of the ham.]

These old hams, they're a pretty significant investment. It's one thing to buy hams in January and sell them a year later and make some money. It's a cycle we're used to. But holding on to them another year…that takes patience. But it's what I like doing now.

Woodlands Pork
Black Oak Holler, West Virginia

Arguably, no aged American ham travels more and hangs longer than a Woodlands Pork Mountain Ham. The brand's heritage-breed hogs are raised in the Appalachian foothills of Black Oak Holler, West Virginia, and then slaughtered in Warsaw, Kentucky. The hams are moved to Broadbent's in Kuttawa, Kentucky, for salting and equalizing. And they're moved yet again to their final resting place, the Cure House in Louisville, Kentucky, a nondescript warehouse on the town's south side. There they'll hang at least two years under the watchful eye of ham maker Jay Denham. [When fully operational in 2014, the Cure House will gain USDA certification, eliminating trips to Broadbent's.]

A longtime fine dining chef, Denham left the restaurant industry in 2008 to advance his charcuterie skills under the guidance of several European masters. During his nine months as an apprentice for curing legends such as Massimo Spigaroli, he lived in a fourteenth-century castle where thousands of prized culatello hams hung in its cellar. He returned to America to create world-class hams with partners Chuck Talbott, a hog geneticist and West Virginia farmer, and investor Nick Heckett.

The idea for Woodlands Pork began with Heckett's desire to import the best prosciutto di Parma hams to America, but he decided against that after learning that he'd have to build a costly USDA-certified facility overseas. After reading about Talbott in Peter Kaminsky's book Pig Perfect, *he tracked down the hog farmer and discussed making hams here. Talbott explained how the Appalachian forest is the world's ideal grazing land for hogs. Its diverse mast [fruits and nuts that fall to the ground from trees] is unrivaled, even in Europe, and the hogs' diet adds incomparable flavor to their meat.*

Mountain Hams aging slowly in Woodlands Pork's modern curing facility.

Woodlands Pork partner and curer Jay Denham prefers to cure whole hog legs, just as he learned while training in Italy.

Jay Denham.

The pitch prompted Heckett to produce the world's finest hams here using Talbott's pork and Denham's curing expertise.

Today, a whole Woodlands Pork Mountain Ham sells for about $350—about as much as six times the cost of some country hams. Much of that expense is tied to Woodlands' investment in its hogs. The rest goes to the time-consuming labor required for Denham's European-style curing process and the company's advanced aging facility. There Denham monitors the meat's pH, encourages and controls natural mold growth and manages the aging house's humidity precisely. Whereas many country ham makers dehumidify their aging rooms, Denham increases humidity to keep more moisture in his hams. Moisture promotes enzymatic activity that creates flavor, which gets distributed more evenly throughout the meat. The longer that activity occurs through careful aging, the greater the ham's flavor complexity and intensity.

"One of our goals is when consumers taste our ham, they can appreciate the life of the pig and the food it ate," Denham says. "That pig had to have a great diet and life, so it can develop and get those great flavors. We're careful to preserve that."

MAYBE THE BEST WAY TO DESCRIBE WHY WE DO THAT IS TO SEE MOISTURE CONTENT INSIDE A HAM AS BOURBON IN A BARREL. It moves around and distributes those flavors over long periods of time and temperature changes. I try to keep

Left: Denham explains why European curers prepare hams with a flat shape.

Below: Contrary to the low humidity sought by most curers, Denham goes the opposite direction in order to maintain moisture.

humidity at around 70 percent, whereas most [country ham makers] try to pull moisture out of the air. When you have less change in water activity, the ham ages longer and becomes extremely flavorful without becoming super salty, which can be a problem with some country hams. You don't want to dry out the outside so quickly that the moisture inside can't escape. So you slowly absorb that salt to the middle, where it hits the bone and works its way back out, moving freely. It's tricky, but I like the challenge.

THE SUMMERTIME HERE IN THE OHIO VALLEY IS THE BEST FOR THIS. When it's hot here, you also have high humidity, so our climate is extremely favorable for producing these kinds of hams…and bourbon. If the humidity gets too low, I use a spray gun—exactly the kind you'd use to paint a car—to humidify the room. Since the humidifiers can't keep up with the demand, I manually introduce it to the air. It's like reproducing the dew that would be on an ambient-cured ham.

MOLD IS WHERE YOU GET MUCH OF THE FLAVOR FROM. It's like making cheese. You want a combination of greens and whites to get those favorable flavor characteristics. And these hams will continue to get better and better over time because of the mold spores in this room. Once they've taken over a room, they'll dominate it and provide that flavor. But you can have bad molds, too. So if we need to remove the air from this room to get rid of that or some bacterial growth, we can flush it all out in about five minutes.

THIS ISN'T YOUR AVERAGE HAM HOUSE. …When this whole place is finished, we'll be able to set a wet and dry bulb temperature for our cure rooms, which will take care of adding or pulling back on moisture automatically. Yeah, some of the old-timers tell me they don't think this is necessary. But if they tasted our ham, they could tell the difference. There's no way they'd miss it. My job is to take old-world curing methods and extend those flavor profiles within the meat through modern methods. We're going to these lengths to create the best pork possible, so I have to get as many flavors out of these hams as possible.

Our hams are flat and shaped like they are so they absorb salt evenly—there's less variation around the ham. The way we break down our pigs is really important. It's a combination of Italian-, Spanish- and American-style butchery. We use saws to split the carcasses, but after that, it's all knife work. Our muscle harvest is a combination of Spanish and Italian cuts, which is different from what you see on other hams.

WHEN I WAS A CHEF, I ALWAYS HAD CURING PROGRAMS IN RESTAURANTS WHERE I WORKED. I had an obsession with taking something fresh and making it for later use. That's real *garde manger*. [A French term, *garde manger* essentially means the preparation of cold foods. Some are simple, such as salads; others are more complex, such as cured proteins and patés.] Cooking is a technical skill, but *garde manger* is more of an art to me because you have to think weeks ahead to get terrines and gravlax and charcuterie ready for later.

I got out of cooking in 2008. I'd already been working on this project [with Talbott and Heckett] indirectly through the restaurant for a while, so when it closed, I had the chance to pursue my passion and went to Europe for nine months.

IN ITALY, I WORKED A LOT WITH MASSIMO SPIGAROLI, a chef [and owner of Antica Corte Pallavicina in Parma, Italy] who also cures hams. That was an amazing experience. I worked several other places, too. It was a great education. The people there welcomed me and were willing to share their knowledge with anyone who really wanted to pursue that craft. Their kids over there are like ours: they don't want to be on the farm; they want to move to cities. So many of the people I saw there working on farms weren't even from Italy. They were Germans and Americans who wanted to get back to that pace of life.

OUR FACILITY IS PRETTY MODERN, AND WE USE A LOT OF EQUIPMENT YOU WON'T SEE IN OTHER OPERATIONS. That's a deboner over there—most everyone still debones their hams by hand—and that's a skinner, and that's for vacuum wrapping. This skinner is wicked. It will take the skin off your own hands in a second if you don't know what you're doing. It's kind of scary. If you look at the names on the equipment, you'll see they're made by Italian, Spanish and German companies mostly. Other than that band saw, we don't make much equipment for this business here in America.

I also play them country music. Yeah, the hams. Sounds crazy, but I guarantee the sound in the room will affect the movement of moisture. It just makes sense. Music affects plants and the moisture that moves inside them, so why wouldn't that sound frequency move the moisture inside hams?

THE HOGS ARE EVERYTHING. Chuck knows so much about them. We've used a lot heritage breeds like Ossabaw and Mulefoot. We have two captive wild boars, Bert and Ernie, who he uses for breeding. You like those names, huh? They're still wild, though. I wouldn't want to be in the pen alone with them.

But even with the great genetics we have, you still have to feed them really well. If you give them crappy feed, genetics won't matter. The flavors of what they eat go into their fat, and the fat is what gives us those incredible flavors in our finished products. And you get that fat into their muscles by letting them get a lot of exercise. That final stage, where we finish them on the forest mast, is so important to creating that intramuscular fat by letting them graze. [To see a compelling video of how Woodlands Pork raises its pigs naturally, visit YouTube and type in "The Curehouse."]

WE PLANT OUR FIELDS WITH WHAT WILL BE THEIR GRAZING FEED, THINGS LIKE BARLEY, RAPE, CORN, BEANS AND SQUASHES. And when they're in the forest in the fall, they eat hickory nuts, papaws, roots, grubs, beechnuts—things you won't find in Europe. We also want our flavors to reflect what they ate in a particular year. So when you have a high nut harvest in one year, we want that to come across in the pork. That's why there's no smoke on our pork. Just salt and time. When we begin packaging slices, we'll even put vintage dates on our packages to reflect that.

Even our forestry program is important. We cull out trees on the farm that aren't producing food for the pigs. Just as soil content is so important to the flavor of grapes used for wine, the same applies to the foods our pigs eat. That's very important to flavor. *Terroir* is hugely important to this. What we're doing is so far beyond just pasture-raising pigs.

No, I have no idea who would want to cook this ham. I hope they don't, because it's not meant for that. I understand why people cook their country ham; a lot of people still can't get past the idea of uncooked pork, even though it's cured and safe to eat. People ate it uncooked for centuries. So if it's really well aged, why do it? I wouldn't. So much of the time and effort put into aging that ham properly changes when you cook it.

WE CALL OURS MOUNTAIN HAM TO DISTINGUISH IT SOME FROM COUNTRY HAM. Country ham has to have a certain percentage of salt within it to be what's technically defined as "country ham." We don't follow that. We're trying to keep the most amount of moisture in there while curing it at a safe level. That doesn't mean I don't have a lot of respect for country ham or the people who make it. There's some really good country ham out there. It just means we're doing something different.

I KNOW WE AREN'T DOING IT LIKE MOST HAM MAKERS HERE, BUT THERE COULD BE NO MORE AMERICAN PRODUCT THAN OURS. Part of what we have to do is educate people that you can't make it more American than we do. That's a big reason why we call it Mountain Ham.

Clifty Farm Country Meats
Paris, Tennessee

Dan Murphey can't precisely say when Clifty Farm Country Hams became an industry giant. His father founded the business in 1954, and it simply never stopped growing. Truman Murphey hung 200 hams that first year and 2,200 a decade later. Today, Clifty Farm produces 750,000 country hams annually—nearly one-third of all country hams made in the United States. Accomplishing that feat requires a 133,000-square-foot complex in Paris, Tennessee, and a 40,000-square-foot curing house in Scottsville, Kentucky.

Much of that growth was spurred by Dan Murphey's work as its soft-spoken TV pitchman. With his grandfatherly persona, Murphey shares family-centered messages and ham cooking tips that have helped the brand become a holiday favorite and a supermarket standard.

Although he's the president of a multimillion-dollar company (he declined to share its revenue), Murphey said that he's still "a peddler at heart" who prefers meeting customers to parsing detailed spreadsheets. At seventy-one, he remains Clifty Farm's key decision-maker while grooming his son, Michael, to take over…someday. "I like what I'm doing well enough to keep at it some more," Murphey said. "But I do miss traveling around in my old car with a trunkload of hams and calling on grocery stores."

As the man in charge, Murphey has had to lead the brand through some tough times. Clifty Farm sued the federal government about thirty years ago over USDA rules that threatened to ruin the business. The USDA backed down. "In a way, we were taking a stand for the country ham industry at that time," Murphey said. "What was good for a company of our size was good for everybody."

M Y FATHER WORKED AT THE TAPPAN APPLIANCE PLANT AS A SUPERVISOR, AND HE WAS TIRED OF WORKING NIGHTS. So he and a friend bought some locker plants in 1954. I bet you don't know what those are, do you? Well, before electricity came around to this area, rural people didn't have freezers. So you could keep your beef and vegetables frozen in a locker until you needed them.

My dad's partner cured some hams, but Dad was so tight that he didn't want to invest in any hams. So his partner financed his first two hundred. Their men would fill up the trunks of their cars with hams, and they'd have a route of grocery stores to call on. Back then, grocery stores didn't use anybody's brand name because they wanted to make people think they were doing all the curing. They also looked down on locker plant hams because they weren't weather cured. They bought them all the same.

When I got out of college in 1964, I got involved in the business, which had grown to about 2,200 hams in the locker plant. The TVA [Tennessee Valley Authority] had come in and people got electricity, so they also got freezers and didn't need locker plants. That was also about the time the USDA had come along and began regulating ham plants. So we converted our locker plant to a federally inspected curing plant.

I TOOK THE BACKSEAT OUT OF A '61 FORD FALCON AND COULD PUT SIXTY HAMS IN BACK OF THAT THING. Back then, hams were a lot smaller, about thirteen pounds cured, which is why I could fit that much. Later, we bought a pickup with a cover on it so I could haul more. I really loved selling hams, loved being a peddler.

We've always tried to keep what we do as close as possible to the old way of curing. We use flake salt that's highly refined because, as I understand it, once the impurities are removed from salt, it has less of a bite. We also blend it with nitrates and nitrites, and we added sugar when we figured out that it toned down the salt taste. And hams marketed as "sugar cured"…well, that's a crock. Sugar doesn't cure. Sugar also gives us more problems with yeast mold than the regular dry mold you find on hams.

Used to be when you salted a ham, you'd start by pushing on the shank end to push that blood out of there. We realized that employees squeeze a lot better at seven in the morning than they do at two in the afternoon, so we bought a piece of equipment from Italy: a combination press-massager. You put the fresh ham through, and it squeezes the blood out and massages it some so it takes the salt better. Using this, four people could put out twenty thousand hams a week—a million hams a year—if that's what we wanted to do. We tried a mechanical salter also, but it didn't work well at all, so we still salt by hand, which I like.

We put salt on in two applications. We let the hams sit in vats as the salt works, and we hold the internal temperature of the hams at 37.5 degrees for fifty days. After that, we wash them and hang them on trees [i.e., hanging racks] in the drying room for equalization. They'll stay in there for three weeks at 60 degrees and with the humidity set at 60 percent. We're more concerned about humidity than temperature, which is why I don't like weather curing. You can't control humidity. After that they go to the smokehouse. Overall, we like to keep them about 120 days, then they're finished.

YEAH, I DO WANT SOME AGE ON MY HAM, BUT I DON'T WANT IT DRIED LIKE SHOE LEATHER EITHER. We like to let them hang thirty days after they've been in the smokehouse, because if you slice it right out of the smoke, it'll taste

Left: Salted and stacked, water will drain from these hams for several weeks.

Below: One of many drying rooms at Clifty Farm. Hams hung on "trees" are easily moved by forklift throughout the facility.

like a salty, tenderized ham. But if you give it that thirty days, you'll have a much better-tasting ham.

We'll sell two-thirds of our hams in the last quarter of the year. But since we can't cure all those at the same time, we'll do it year round and put a lot of them in the freezer. If we're going to hold them, we like to freeze them right out of the smokehouse because that enzyme is [still active] in the freezer.

We've grown pretty steady through the years. By the time we built out here, we were curing about 48,000 hams a year. The most we ever cured was in 2000, when we cured 900,000. That was a busy year. And I know that sounds like a lot, but let me put that into perspective first: There are 470,000 hogs killed every day in this country, so one day's slaughter could furnish our biggest year. That boggles my mind. When you look at it like that, we're a small frog in a huge pond. But when you look at just country ham, we're a big frog in a little-bitty pond. [Note: According to 2012 data from the USDA, the average daily hog slaughter count is closer to 317,000, a number that accounts only for hogs processed for retail (i.e., officially taxable) purposes.]

The reason we were so busy that year was [because] Kroger Louisville, which had about eighty-five stores in its division back then, wanted to do a Meat Madness sale in October. They were going to sell them at ninety-nine cents a pound, though we were selling ours to them at $1.04 a pound, so it was a loss leader. They first wanted eighteen to twenty loads, which is 2,500 hams per truckload. [A truckload weighs forty thousand pounds.] When they called and said they wanted thirty loads, that made me nervous. When that sale hit, they were calling for extra loads. We had to cut them off because we have other customers to service. We've never commited to just one. They ended up selling 106,000 hams in four days.

Some might look at that and say a big company like ours is hurting the small ones by doing that. I don't agree. I believe that what's good for Clifty Farm is good for the industry. A sale like that raises awareness of country ham. Bill Robertson [former owner of Finchville Farms Country Ham] and I are good buddies, and he said to me back then, "When they came out with that sale, I thought we'd not sell another ham this year. But we had the best year!" See what I mean? It helped others.

The lawsuit with the government is another example. It benefitted everybody for us to stand up and say to those inspectors, "We've run our company this way for a long time, and you're not going to tell us to change that." The lawsuit was back in the early '80s, and it came when a question arose over the correct temperature for smoking hams.

There were some companies [in North Carolina] running their hams through the [curing and aging] process in about ninety days. That's real fast. North Carolina had some political pull, and a senator from there got the USDA to change the regulation for smoking country hams. It said you couldn't heat them over ninety-five degrees. Well, in a west Tennessee summer, it's ninety-five degrees just outside. And if you smoke at eighty-five degrees, it doesn't work anyway; it's too cool, and the ham gets streaky and looks awful because it won't accept the color.

We started calling around at the USDA about the rule, but we couldn't find anyone who knew how that change got passed. Everybody there said they didn't do it, but they knew that was the rule. When they started hiring local inspectors to come check out our smokehouse temperatures to make sure they didn't get over ninety-five degrees, we'd had enough. We filed suit against them in federal court in Jackson, Tennessee.

The USDA claimed it had done a survey [of country ham makers] who said they didn't smoke above ninety-five degrees. We didn't believe them, so we asked for a copy of it, but they couldn't find the survey. So, under the Freedom of Information Act, we got all the documents we could, but we never found that survey. The USDA knew it was in a corner on this one.

My lawyer said the USDA told him they'd not enforce that rule on us if we'd just drop our case. I said, "You got that in writing from them?" He didn't, and so I wasn't buying it. What would happen is somebody there can say they're not enforcing it one day, but the next day a new inspector says, "This is the rule." I wasn't dealing with that.

I called the administrator at the USDA myself and asked if he'd give me what my lawyer said in writing. Well, he got flustered and hung up. Then I got a call from my lawyer, who said, "You're not supposed to be calling them and saying that!" But I told him that *this was my livelihood, that I have to know what's going on at every level*. I wasn't going to just take anyone's word for it.

They wanted us to drop the case, but we wouldn't, and it finally goes to court [in Jackson]. We had our attorney, and they had about seven government attorneys. One of theirs was a lawyer from Philadelphia, an impressive man in a three-piece suit. He gets up and tells everyone he's a friend of court representing the American Association of Meatpackers…and he gets about two sentences out before the judge said, "Why is someone from Philadelphia coming to west Tennessee to tell anybody about country ham?"

And the guy just closed his folder and sat down! My attorney and I thought that was a good one!

When a woman from the USDA spoke, we could tell she had no idea what she was talking about. The USDA didn't know the country ham business, but they presented all they had, which didn't amount to much, then we presented all we had.

THE JUDGE PUT AN INJUNCTION ON THE USDA RULE AND TOLD THEM THEY HAD THIRTY DAYS TO RESPOND. We knew the government was tickled that they'd lost because they wanted to be out of the whole mess anyway. They knew all they had to do then was go back to the senator who'd pushed it through and say that they couldn't enforce it.

Our inspector didn't know about the ruling, and so he was still there, probing our hams every day and checking temperatures. I called him into my office and said, "This is an injunction against that regulation, and I don't want you probing another ham here for thirty days." He said he'd not heard a word about it yet, so I told him, "This is a court order, and if you probe another ham here, I'll have a federal marshal up here so fast it'll make your head swim." I wanted them to understand that they weren't going to run this place.

MAYBE I GREW UP IN THE WRONG GENERATION, BUT I WAS TOLD THAT THE GOVERNMENT WAS SUPPOSED TO BE YOUR FRIEND, THAT IT WAS HERE TO HELP YOU. This wasn't the case, and I really got cynical from all this. But we're still here, doing mostly what we've always done and getting along pretty well.

Not everything about the business has changed since I started, but a lot has. A lot of country ham makers want out of the whole ham business because sliced is about the only way they can sell it. Whole hams are what we built the company on, and that's what I like to sell. Our plant in Kentucky will do 250,000 to 300,000 whole hams a year with a dozen men. That's a whole lot easier than all this processing. We still sell more whole hams than sliced, but that's dwindling every year.

SO WE'VE DIVERSIFIED SOME. LIKE A LOT OF OTHERS, WE'VE GOT BACON AND SAUSAGE. BUT WE'VE ALSO ADDED BARBECUE—PULLED PORK AND RIBS. They've done really well for us. No, I don't think that's the future for us, at least not while I'm here. The industry doesn't change that fast, and I'm getting up there in years. I think country ham as our big product will outlive me. I'm pretty confident of that.

CHAPTER 4

THE FUTURE OF COUNTRY HAM, FORETOLD BY CHEFS

When Allan Benton bought his country ham business in 1970s, he vowed to make his ham the finest available. But when he started hawking them to chefs in nearby Tennessee tourist areas, they wanted cheap pork, not premium pig.

Unwilling to lower his standards, he targeted a more receptive audience and called on Bob Carter, then executive chef at the ultra-exclusive Blackberry Farm resort in Walland, Tennessee. When Carter recognized Benton's ham for the treasure it was, Benton saw the future for his operation. "Once I got selling to restaurants…that changed my business because I believed serious chefs understood country ham," Benton recalled. "Not everyone in that business wanted mine, which is fine, but I believed there were more who did."

Nancy Newsom's story is similar, as is Bob Woods's, Sam Edwards's and Jay Denham's—all ham makers who've realized that a significant portion of their companies' future sales rest in the hands of chefs who view country ham on par with Europe's finest cured flanks. They know that country ham is served charcuterie style in better restaurants, not awash in red-eye gravy.

"Customers are seeing it not just as hillbilly food," Woods said. "They know it's something out of the ordinary, and they like that it comes from here."

Ironically, that change in customer perception appears nearly glacial in the South. Below the Ohio River, country ham primarily is a breakfast food bookended by biscuit halves, sliced as a thin steak or a holiday centerpiece that's boiled, baked and served whole. And why not, when most country ham makers don't eat their products au naturel? The thought makes Ginny

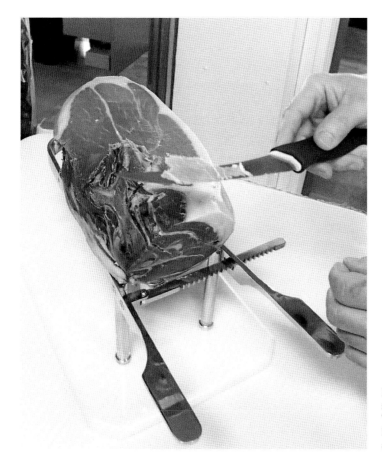

Bob Woods
slices a
Tennshootoe
ham for
charcuterie.

Dabbs close her eyes and faux-shiver. "I guess I can see how people might like it…but noooo…not for me," she said. "We don't market ours that way, though there probably are people who eat them like that."

"And they aren't me," husband Scott Dabbs added, half-grinning. "Nope."

Brian Harper has eaten it uncooked, but he said, "It's not as good as cooked. To me anyway." Same for June Scott. "Maybe it's all in my head, but it's, just, well, pork that's not cooked. I know they say it's safe, but that doesn't change it for me. I know we have customers who eat it like that, though, and that's okay. We're just happy they enjoy it."

Technically, the USDA agrees with those who think it should always be cooked, saying that country ham can't be marketed as "ready to eat." Yet prosciutto, though dry-cured virtually identically (salt only, no sugar, other spice or smoke), *can* be marketed "ready to eat."

The difference comes down to water activity, which is a measure of "free water" within cured meat that could lend support to microbial growth. Without digging too deeply into the complex science behind it, water activity in prosciutto is commonly 0.85, while in country ham it's 0.88. Yep, that's the USDA dividing line, a difference of 0.03.

"What's a little aggravating is we could certify our hams ready to eat without any doubt, but the testing process is pretty expensive," said Ronnie Drennan. He said he talked about doing that with several other ham makers, "but we didn't think it was worth it. So we just keep the warning on the label that it should be cooked."

Tyler Brown, executive chef at The Capitol Grille in Nashville, Tennessee, said that he's surprised so few ham makers have joined the ranks of the room-temperature charcuterie crowd. Ignoring country ham's potential served just as it is to better restaurants is costing curers sales to chefs who will pay top dollar, he said. "You talk to some of them, and they don't believe there's any credence to the idea of selling to better places. And they can't see it until they take that leap," said Brown, whose restaurant is located in the historic Hermitage Hotel. "You can't show them the money they're going to make until they put themselves out there."

Country ham is always featured on the Grille's menu in multiple ways, but most prominently on its charcuterie plate. The appetizer includes slices from several regional ham makers like Benton's, The Hamery and Newsom's. By serving a variety, Brown said, he subtly exposes customers to different styles and brands. "There's always going to be a group that says country ham is too salty or too dry," Brown said. "But country ham isn't something you eat a lot of or even eat every day. We have a hard time with moderation in this culture. We should look at that and consider that country ham is maybe a once-a-month thing."

Jay Denham suspects that some might cook his Woodlands Pork Mountain Ham, but he doesn't know why, especially when his hams start at $300 each. The mere thought of cooking it brings a puzzled look to his face. "We take so much time aging these hams to keep moisture in them. That's the whole point," he said. "So why would you want to cook it out?" he said.

At the 2014 StarChefs Rising Star Awards Gala in Louisville, Denham sliced and served one of his aged hams at room temperature. The pile of maroon ribbons of meat streaked with ivory fat drew a constant stream of attendees to his table throughout the evening. "That's how it's done in Europe. Slice it. Done," Denham said. "Once you heat something, you change textures and flavors that you get only through curing."

In other words, to know what something really tastes like, it must be consumed unadorned (i.e. sipping tequila straight rather than cloaking it in a margarita or eating cheese sliced from a room-temperature block, not cut, packaged and chilled). To taste Mountain Ham simply sliced, Denham said, is to taste what that pig ate and how it lived.

"If you cook it, you're melting out most of the fat that holds all those flavors," he said. Even Denham's bacon—whose meat is luminously red against its snow-white fat—is cured for uncooked consumption. "Why else would we take all the time we do to feed our pigs so well when they're alive if we didn't want to promote great flavor in our ham?"

Author Peter Kaminsky, a New Yorker familiar with the virtues of prosciutto *crudo* (Italian for "uncooked"), admits that he once cooked his country ham. "When I started buying [Newsom's] hams, I'd simmer them in apple cider for two and a half hours," he said. "That's good, but it's not the same as just slicing it."

Kaminsky is optimistic that southerners eventually will come to appreciate country ham served just sliced. Even humble immigrant foods, such as pizza and tacos, took time to become national favorites. "Look how quickly tacos moved into the mainstream," he began. "Americans are drinking espresso and macchiato now? If you'd have told me that forty years ago they'd be doing that, I'd have laughed at you. It just depends on when a thing catches fire and how it catches fire."

In San Francisco, where customers of Hog & Rocks don't arrive with preconceptions about country ham, people eat uncooked ribbons of it without thinking, "This should have been fried and there should be some grease on the plate," said Executive Chef Robin Song. Without having been to a country ham dinner or seeing it tucked into a warm biscuit, Song said that Californians easily accept it sliced and served. "We offer it as prosciutto-style ham, so that's how they consume it. The country ham you're talking about doesn't resonate with them. In that way, it's good that they don't know the difference."

Song favors "hyper-local ingredients" for his menus, but since no one cures ham in California, he makes a broader search of American sources to fill the gaps. "If we want charcuterie, the obvious choice is to use European hams, but I like domestic products," said Song, who also sells European cured hams. "When the closest thing to domestic ham is the guys down south making it, that answers the question of, 'What is American ham?'"

It's cured ham that's smoked, Song added, and it's that smoky flavor that differentiates his American selections from his European cuttings. "The salty

Walter Bundy, executive chef at Lemaire in Richmond, Virginia. *Courtesy of Hayes and Fisk Photography.*

ham thing is big out here, and I love prosciuttos and serranos," Song began. "But I love the smoke. Love it! I smoke a lot of my food because it gives a fantastic flavor profile, a lot of depth. You get that in country ham and really good smoked bacon."

Walter Bundy also is a smoke fan, and he uses country ham as a flavor accent in several dishes he cooks at Lemarie, where he's executive chef. "I use it pretty much all the time," said Bundy, whose restaurant is located in the Jefferson Hotel in Richmond, Virginia. "It's like bacon in that it brings so much flavor to a dish."

Bundy serves slices of Edwards Surryano ham over Black Mission figs, roasted red peppers and arugula. He also dices Kite's Country Ham into a dish of roasted mussels and even cantaloupe bisque with mint. "Southern food like country ham is real food, real *American* food," Bundy said. "A lot of our food in the South tells a story. For me, ham sings a song of the South. It makes you glad to be alive and to appreciate the craftsmanship that went into making that product."

Woods said he used to be narrow-mindedly confident that country hams were for country folk only, sliced for biscuits and fried for platters. But after seeing the work of chefs like Bundy and the prices charged for aged

European hams, he was convinced that he should try long-aging some hams and offering them to fine dining restaurants for charcuterie.

Today, sales to everything from white tablecloth restaurants to wood-fired pizzerias are a growing portion of his business. "Were I forty-two—I'm sixty-two now—I'd tackle that world because I think there's a lot of potential there," said Woods. "I love going in the back door of these restaurants and saying, 'I've got a ham I think you ought to try.'"

Much of Michael Paley's career as a chef was steeped in the Italian tradition, and that kept him using prosciutto only. When he moved to Louisville to open Proof on Main in 2009, he was amazed at the abundance of locally grown foods, things he rarely had access to even in Florida. Shortly afterward, he tasted Newsom's aged ham, and it stopped him. It tasted like prosciutto with a kiss of smoke. "I knew it should be served like charcuterie," Paley said.

In 2011, when he opened Garage Bar, he insisted that the restaurant have a country ham and oyster bar. There patrons can sit and watch cooks slice see-through ribbons of ham on manually operated flywheel slicer. On each platter are piled tufts of sliced ham from Benton's, Newsom's, Meacham Country Hams (in Sturgis, Kentucky) or Broadbent's beside a sliced baguette and a ramekin of red-eye aioli. The creamy, gray-white dressing is made with an emulsion of eggs, olive oil, shallots and pan drippings from cooked country ham. "I love prosciutto, but I wanted domestic products that weren't so expensive," said Paley. "Nancy actually came up here to train our staff on how to sell it and talk about how she made it."

Paley said that he used Newsom's two-year-old ham until demand for the product made it difficult to get—a situation not unique since only a handful of curers age hams beyond a year. Since ham makers don't always share their business details, it's difficult to tally how many long-age hams smaller artisans keep on hand. My own best estimate is 20,000 or less—a fraction of the 2.5 million or so country hams cured each year in the United States. That tight supply of long-aged hams is leading chefs like Brown to consider curing his own.

"That idea is as exciting to me," said Brown, who, along with several Hermitage staffers, works the Farm at Glen, a sizeable piece of land outside Nashville where much of the restaurant's produce and beef cattle are raised. His toil in the soil has earned him the nickname "Farmer Brown." "I'd like to do a smokehouse where we're raising our cattle. Carrying on that tradition of putting up hams, I can see that happening for sure."

Hog & Rocks' Song said that plans are in the works to build a curing room that he'd share with the company's sister restaurant, Hi-Lo, a barbecue spot. "That's a goal of ours for sure," he said. "We'd love to do our own."

Kitt Garrett and Bob Hancock, owners, Blue Dog Bakery, Louisville, Kentucky.

Blue Dog Bakery owners Bob Hancock and Kitt Garrett manage the complete cycle: they raise fifty heritage-breed pigs, cure their hams and serve them at the Louisville breakfast-and-lunch spot.

As Hancock began studying curing several years ago, he learned more about the mistreatment of pigs reared and slaughtered in factory operations and vowed, "I'm not going to be involved in that. But I knew there wasn't a way to be sure that wasn't happening to the meat I was going to cure unless I knew exactly how the pig was treated."

Starting with a few hogs, the couple increased their drove to the point they could begin slaughtering for hams. The lessons that followed didn't come easily. "I made some mistakes in the beginning," Hancock said. "I've always done mine inside, and in the beginning, I didn't have the best temperature controls."

After correcting his methods and aging some quality hams, he started a Red Hog Tapas night at the bakery featuring a range of appetizers made from his cured meats. The sold-out events were so successful that they've been halted temporarily.

Hancock likes to talk curing, but the conversation inevitably winds back to his pigs, animals he and Garrett talk about like family. Their eight-hundred-pound Red Wattle pigs are surprisingly friendly, especially when fed their evening treat of fruits, veggies and bread scraps from the bakery. Their Mulefoot hogs, which are equally engaging, are being crossbred with the Red Wattles for temperament, health and meat characteristics.

Hancock's not crazy about sending them off for slaughter, but he acknowledges it as part of the cycle. So when it's time for the hogs to go, he travels with them, unloads them personally and spends an hour or two inside the holding pen helping them relax. "I scratch them behind the ears to calm them down," he said. "If the animal is stressed, it's going to affect the meat, and I don't want that in our hams."

Later, he feeds them their last meal and then spends the night at a nearby hotel so he can see them once more in the morning. "I figure I owe that much to them seeing as what they're giving up for us," he said. "But it's also one more thing I can do to make sure that meat's good. That's important."

CHAPTER 5

CURE YOURSELF

MAKING YOUR OWN COUNTRY HAM

I can tell you how to cure a ham, but you can't do it.
—Ed Rice, owner, Rice's Country Hams

Despite Ed Rice's discouraging statement, curing a fresh ham to an edible, shelf-stable state is fairly simple. Were it not, humans would have skipped curing and stuck with cooking long ago.

What Rice really means is that curing is best learned by observation and by spending a full curing cycle in the ham house watching, touching and smelling—especially smelling, he stresses. Seeing that meat change shape and color over many months is the best way to master the task, and the surest way to learn is to do it yourself.

If you follow the directions in this chapter, your first hams are likely to turn out well—probably not as good as Rice's initially, but tasty enough that you'll do it the next year. And when that next year comes and mold appears, you won't be alarmed. During the stretch between spring equalization and the summer sweat, you'll know that odor emanating from the smokehouse isn't rot—it's just the funky-fine byproduct of favorable, flavorful fermentation.

You'll know a little bit more about whether it's better to smoke on rainy or dry days, or only in the spring and never in the summer, because you'll have done it. Knowledge is the product of experience, and as Rice said, written instructions can't beat "being in that smokehouse every day, trying to see what's different and learning from it."

Salted, peppered and stacked, hams are cured year round at Benton's Smoky Mountain Country Hams.

What Rice knows and amateurs don't is the hundred reasons why our hams won't taste like his or any other curers' interviewed for this book. For example, Colonel Bill Newsom told his daughter, Nancy, "Every ham house has its own mold," meaning that where a ham is aged plays a significant role in its flavor. Weather has a profound effect on ambient-cured meats, and Kentucky's climate is different from that of Tennessee's, Virginia's, North Carolina's or Missouri's.

If you want to try curing a ham, just do it. The craft was performed successfully for centuries without the benefits of mechanical refrigeration and nitrates that ensure a safer cure. As you'll see in the following instructions, curing isn't terribly hard if you commit to purchasing a few tools of the craft and stick with a reliable plan. Although access to a smokehouse is ideal (there are a number of smokehouse plans available for free on the Internet), a whole ham or two will fit neatly into a larger smoker with an offset or external firebox to provide cool smoke.

Curing, like cooking, takes practice, so make notes along the way to document your procedure and progress throughout the curing cycle. It'll help you recall what went well and what didn't and better prepare you for the next try. If you're fortunate enough to know experienced curers, ask lots of questions. Most are more than willing to share with another hobbyist. If possible, consult them before you get started.

Use online discussion forums, such as www.smokingmeatforums.com, and check out the growing number of ham curing videos on YouTube. One of the most helpful is a video done by the University of Kentucky's Gregg Rentfrow on what's called an "in-bag cure method." I don't detail that here, but much of his procedure is similar enough to the "box-cure method" that a quick viewing is instructive. If for no other reason than seeing how simple it is, it's worth watching.

The following is a blend of instructions I've read on curing gained during my research for this book. Many of the basics come from Rentfrow's copious instructions. The numerous tips sprinkled throughout are from the veterans profiled in this book.

Supplies

- knife
- cure (salt, sugar, spices and nitrates—mix of all or some)
- cotton or poly stockinettes (found at www.home-processor.com)
- smokehouse and/or ham house
- scale (optional)
- green ham

The Ham

"Green" is an industry term describing a freshly harvested ham; it has nothing to do with color. Factory-produced green hams weigh about twenty-three pounds and, like all hams, should be cured as quickly as possible after slaughter. When I told Nancy Newsom that I had a pair of five-day-old hams, she winced. "I don't like to go much longer than two days if I can avoid it," she said.

Later, when I learned that my hams were frozen, she and several other curers said not to use them. Jay Denham said that the ice crystals inside the ham would leave too much water inside the musculature when thawed. "Bacteria love water," he said.

It's unlikely you'll find fresh green hams at an ordinary supermarket. Expect to order one from a good butcher shop and plan to cure it immediately. If you can purchase hams from a local farm, it's likely that they'll send that hog to a USDA-certified processing operation before returning the ham to you. Instruct them to not freeze the ham, then schedule a prompt pickup and cure it immediately.

Preparing the Ham

Use a sharp boning knife to cut away any loose skin or fat. This gives the ham a smooth look once it's finished curing, and it removes flesh that might block the cure from contacting the meat directly.

Employees at Clifty Farm can cure as many as twenty thousand hams a week working as a team. Here they rub fresh hams in a blend of flake salt, sugar and nitrates.

The Cure

Unless you're using salt only, no two professional ham makers use the same cure. Many curers do start with a base of 80 percent salt and 20 percent brown sugar, while adding various amounts of spices such as black pepper, crushed red pepper or paprika. (Some say that they can taste pepper in the final product, while others say they can't. All agree that pepper helps repel insects.) Rentfrow's recipe, following, covers four to five average-size hams weighing one hundred pounds total.

Recipe

8 pounds of curing salt (not iodized salt; curing salt can be found at
 outdoors stores and online)
2 pounds of white or brown sugar (most use brown)

ADDED TO PREFERENCE:
black pepper
red pepper
paprika
nitrate and/or nitrite (Prague powder, saltpeter, Instacure #2™),
 used according to manufacturer's guidelines

Home curers don't have to use nitrates or nitrites. Some just want an all-
natural cure, while others don't want the flavor nitrates and nitrites add to
cured meat. (Some can taste them, others can't.) They also redden the color
of cured meat, which is off-putting to some. Still, many of the finest country
ham makers use nitrates and/or nitrites.

*Note: Should you use nitrates or nitrites, do so exactly to the manufacturer's guidelines.
Excess amounts are unsafe for human consumption.*

Curing and Stacking

Ham makers following an ambient method rely on the weather to cool,
warm and ultimately sweat their hams in step with the changing seasons. To
preserve the meat, the process must start when daytime high temperatures
are lower than forty degrees Fahrenheit. In most of the Country Ham Belt,
it's best to start between December and February.

 Choose a washable plastic container large enough to hold several pounds
of cure and a single ham. Scoop up handfuls of cure and rub vigorously
onto every surface of the ham. Pack cure into any exposed bones or joints.
It is especially important that the hock end of the ham (a.k.a. the shank) is
packed full of cure.

 Note that you won't use all the cure for this first application, so don't
be concerned when at least half remains in your container. Store the cure

covered in a container until the next salting, about seven to ten days later. Once your green hams are covered in cure, Rentfrow recommends placing them in a well-drained container made of any material as long as it allows for drainage. As you can see in photos in this section, some large-scale curers use deep plastic totes or vats.

Without such containers at our disposal, my friend and I stacked ours in a refrigerator in his garage, which, as expected, resulted in water leaching out from the hams and dripping onto the garage floor. Messy as that was, the cured hams drained. Note that if you are curing multiple hams,

At large-scale operations like Clifty Farm, hams are held in curing vats as the salt penetrates the meat.

stack each with its hock pointed the opposite direction of the one next to it, nesting them next to one another. If you have enough for two layers, stack them in the opposite direction as you add layers.

Come time for the second application of cure, apply the cure again as done the first time, but restack each ham by rotating it 180 degrees from its original position to help the meat maintain a rounder shape. According to Rentfrow, once applied, the cure penetrates the ham about one inch per week, meaning a seven-inch-thick ham (measured at its thickest portion) would take seven weeks to cure. Curers I talked to kept their hams in cure for shorter spans of thirty to forty days.

Washing

Once a ham is cured, any residual salt should be rinsed off with cold water. This can be done in a large kitchen sink or outside in a container deep enough to hold the ham and water for cleaning it. If washing multiple hams this way, change the water frequently.

Hanging

Starting at the hock (or shank) end, place a plastic or cotton stockinette over the meat with the seam directly at the bottom of the hock. Tie the top end closed and hang the ham, hock down, in the smokehouse. Stainless steel ham hooks, available online, are easiest to use, but many curers use zip ties or bailing twine looped through the stockinette and hung over a nail in the smokehouse. Hams can be hung close together but not touching.

Aging

Salt migration occurs slowly during cold weather. Should an unseasonable warm spell occur and last more than a few days, Rentfrow recommends checking the internal temperature of the ham at its thickest portion. If it's higher than forty-five degrees Fahrenheit, one could move the ham to a refrigerator during the daytime and back outside at night.

"Although the daytime temperature during winter can reach greater than fifty-five degrees Fahrenheit, nighttime temperatures will decrease to safe curing levels," Rentfrow said. "Normally, due to the mass of the ham, the internal temperature will not fluctuate very much, until there are several days above fifty-five degrees Fahrenheit."

Finchville Farms' Bill Robertson said that such warm spells rarely concern him. The sheer, meaty mass of forty thousand cold hams hanging side by side in the company's four ham houses minimizes temperature fluctuations. "I rarely think much about that," he said. "It all works out on its own usually."

After curing, hams are washed clean of excess salt and allowed to dry and equalize before smoking.

Equalization

Equalization is the period when salt migrates evenly throughout the ham as daytime highs rise to fifty or sixty degrees Fahrenheit. As temperatures rise farther, salt migration quickens.

Smoking

Ideally, country hams are cold-smoked at temperatures between 90 and 100 degrees Fahrenheit. If the smoke becomes too hot (110 degrees Fahrenheit), it will destroy enzymes responsible for a ham's flavor, tenderness and aroma.

How long a ham should be smoked is a matter of personal preference. According to Rentfrow, most are smoked twelve hours or more, but Sam

At Clifty Farm's massive facility, thousands of hams are smoked together. The hickory smoke is difficult to see in this picture, but its browning influence on the meat is obvious.

Wallace smokes his for a week. Charlie Gatton of Father's Country Hams smokes ninety-six hours, and Nancy Newsom smokes hers on and off over a period of as many as three weeks, depending on the weather. "I don't see smoke adding any flavor at all," Robertson said. "It's just color, so we don't do it."

Hams should be smoked only using hard woods such as hickory, cherry, apple or maple. (Soft woods such as pine produce bitter flavors, so avoid them.) Some curers use hickory sawdust exclusively or a mix of hickory sawdust, dried and green hickory logs. Scott Hams' Leslie and June Scott add a few green sassafras branches to their fires.

For the smoke to cool by the time it reaches the ham, it should come from an indirect source, such as a firebox outside a smokehouse or on the side of a small smoker. The distance gives the smoke a chance to cool before it gets to the meat, and it greatly reduces the chance that melting ham fat will drip onto the fire source. Such flare-ups can not only ruin good hams, they can also cause destructive fires.

Gatton and Newsom build fires outside the smokehouse in large iron kettles, which they then wheel inside. More modern operations like Broadbent's, Harper's and Clifty Farm use automatic smoke generators that feed hickory sawdust onto an electrically heated metal plate. If the smoke gets too warm, a thermostat shuts off the generator until it cools.

Most smoke their hams until they achieve a desired color. Some prefer them golden brown, others like a mahogany tint and still others are partial to a red-brown or sienna shade.

The Summer Sweat

Here's where the real magic happens. The Country Ham Belt's sultry summers develop complex flavors and aromas by pulling moisture out of the meat. That dehydration—which according to the USDA must be a minimum of 18 percent, although some curers push it to 25 percent—intensifies flavor and firms texture. Old-timers call this stage the "summer sweat" because that's what hams (and ham curers, for that matter) do during this period. As Rentfrow writes, "The longer the hams age, the more intense the flavor of the ham," which is why many prefer older hams.

The summers of 2011 and 2012 brought droughts to Kentucky, which Robertson said robbed his hams of moisture and cut the business's profit margins due to lost product weight. Yet he stressed, "Those were some of the best-tasting hams! It's kind of exciting to see what you're going to get year to year."

Newsom likens the year-to-year difference in ambient-cured hams to variances in wine vintages. "Every year's a little different, which I think gives each ham its own character," she said.

Not everyone agrees with them, especially those who cure year round. Climate-controlled ham plants are designed to mimic the seasons and control evaporation. The result is their hams taste the same each year. "It's really what the market wants," Drennan said. "People want us to be reliable."

By and large, whether hams are control cured or ambient cured, most commercial hams are aged for six to twelve months. Rice said that as a ham passes that half-year mark, "You really notice a change with every month. And if you're in that ham house as much as we are, you can notice changes every week."

Although a country ham is safely cured and edible after four months, most experts recommend waiting. Even at six months, a ham's texture can be spongy and gummy and its flavor underdeveloped. Further aging is recommended to refine the ham.

The Drennans and the Scotts prefer them at nine to ten months, while Rice and his son-in-law, Dabbs, say that the ideal ham is ten to twelve months old. For cooking her ham, Newsom prefers year-old hams, but she's fondest of the complex flavors found in her two-year-olds (as are her many chef clients). Allan Benton likes his twenty-month ham the best, and Denham, who ages his hams in humid conditions, has several three-year-olds in storage; some are closing in on year four.

Mold Growth

The Country Ham Belt's warm temperatures and high humidity develop flavor without robbing the meat of too much moisture. Yet that climate also promotes mold growth. There's no reason to fear ham mold since it's harmless and can be scrubbed off. According to Rentfrow, controlled curers maintain lower relative humidity of 60 percent or less inside to limit mold growth and avoid tedious and costly scrubbing. Ambient curers, however, have little control over humidity other than ensuring good air circulation via proper smokehouse venting and auxiliary fans stirring the air inside.

According to Rentfrow, some curers wipe a light coating of cooking oil onto their hams before the summer sweat to retard mold growth. Interestingly, many old-timers and aficionados actually prefer a moldy ham for the unique flavors imparted. When many of Newsom's hams approach the two-year-old mark, they are covered in a layer of mold that author Peter Kaminsky likened to a foamy head of beer. Tony Holland, the champion amateur curer mentioned in the second chapter, said that one of the best-tasting hams he ever cured was so "white with mold it looked like a ghost."

Benton served me a few slices of fifteen-month-old ham; the mold left an interesting tangy note in the meat. "Some people really like that," he said, "but it's not for everyone. Some also believe that flavor is stronger because we sprinkle our hams with some red pepper. But what's really interesting to me is that flavor ages out and softens when the hams get to twenty months. I have no idea why that happens, but I really like it."

The best way to remove mold is with a brush dipped in a solution of mild vinegar and warm water. If your sink is deep enough, keep the ham under running water while you scrub. Rentfrow said that some molds will leave black dots that are nearly impossible to remove, but like the mold itself, they're harmless. Once the ham's skin is removed for eating, it's gone for good.

Insects and Rodents

Insects and rodents are among the stiffest challenges faced when curing meats in a noncommercial setting. (Even some ambient curers admit that the dreadful pests make a great case for indoor controlled curing.) Every seam of an ambient-cure smokehouse must be properly caulked or mortared or its vents and screen doors covered with fine mesh (32 mesh or smaller). Otherwise, insects and rodents are likely to find their way to the meat and begin their slow, deliberate and damaging feast. Some of the peskiest bugs include the following.

LARDER BEETLES: Colored dark brown to black with a wide cream or tan band with spotted wings. Adults are ¼- to ⅝-inch long. Their larvae, which cause the most damage, are tan and dark brown to black striped and have a fuzzy appearance. They feed just below the surface, causing mostly cosmetic damage that should be trimmed and discarded.

HAM MITES: The most common insect found on dry-cured hams, cause only cosmetic damage, which can be trimmed off. The microscopic mites are difficult to see but leave a telltale white powder on an infested ham. *Nastiness alert*: The powder is a waste product of the mites. According to Rentfrow, a minty odor is evident with extreme infestations.

SKIPPERS AND/OR CHEESE SKIPPERS: Ever the cut-up, Ed Rice said, "For years, we hung a sign in our smokehouse that read, 'No skippers allowed.' But we took it down when we figured out a lot of them couldn't read." Skippers are smaller than houseflies and have black bodies and red eyes. They lay their eggs on the surface of the ham, and their maggots burrow inside to feed. If caught soon enough, the ham can be eaten after removing the bugs, but if not, most curers pitch it. "Skippers can eat so much of the insides that they'll just leave the skin hanging there," Rice said. "They're just awful." The only FDA- and USDA-approved chemicals for use on country hams are methyl bromide and sulfuryl floride (sold under the name Profume). Chemicals can be avoided by freezing a ham after a surface infestation.

With their keen sense of smell, rodents will locate your hams, but proper precautions can secure your smokehouse and ensure that they don't reach them. Place traps along smokehouse walls and check for victims regularly. Clean traps immediately to prevent contamination.

Discourage pests by keeping the floors clean. During the sweat, some ham makers place flattened cardboard boxes under their ham racks to catch drips and reduce the need for floor cleaning. Keep the area outside the smokehouse neat, too, Rentfrow said. High grass and trashy clutter provide cover for sneaky pests.

The End of Aging

If you salted your ham in January, cured and smoked it correctly and won the bug battle, you'll likely have a flavorful ham come September. If you cured multiple hams, consider tasting one. If you like country ham uncooked, then

Finished hams in store at Scott Hams. Every curer has a color preference; the Scotts like a pecan tone.

cut back some of the tough exterior and, with a sharp knife, and shave off a few paper-thin slices. If you're happy with the flavor and texture, then slice and share.

If not, let it age some more inside the house. Now that the ham is cut, insects will be drawn to the open spot. Patch it over with a sheet of plastic film and hang in a cool, dry place. No refrigeration necessary. How is that possible? The curing process creates a drier, saltier meat that creates a hostile environment for germs. As Rentfrow puts it, "country hams are a bacterial desert that cannot support life." And that's good for your life!

CHAPTER 6

TIME TO COOK

COUNTRY HAM RECIPES

The following recipes have been shared by a host of generous ham curers, chefs and home cooks.

In and Out Country Ham Cheddar Omelet (from Tim Laird)

Tim Laird has one of the coolest jobs ever created. As chief entertainment officer for Brown-Forman Corp., owner of such iconic brands as Jack Daniel's Tennessee Whiskey, Woodford Reserve Bourbon, Old Forester Bourbon, Herradura Tequila and Finlandia Vodka, he travels the world showing people how to eat and drink better.

INGREDIENTS
2 slices country ham, about ½ ounce each
3 eggs
pinch kosher salt [do not need much given the country ham]
¼ teaspoon freshly ground black pepper
2 tablespoons heavy cream
2 teaspoons unsalted butter
1 tablespoon green onions, chopped
2 tablespoons mild cheddar cheese, shredded

PROCEDURE

Heat country ham slices in a small skillet over medium heat just until browned, 1 to 2 minutes per side. Remove from heat and dice one slice into small pieces and set aside with the other slice.

In medium bowl, whisk together eggs, salt, pepper and heavy cream until well incorporated. In an 8-inch nonstick skillet, melt butter over medium-high heat. Add egg mixture and stir lightly until just set on the bottom, about 30 seconds. Sprinkle diced ham and green onions over omelet and continue cooking up to 1 minute. When eggs are nearly set, reduce heat to low, sprinkle cheese onto omelet and cover with lid to help cheese melt, about 20 seconds. Fold cooked omelet onto plate and garnish with additional chopped green onions.

Serve with the other country ham slice on the side.

Scrambled Eggs with Country Ham, Spinach and Jalapeños

Trust me on this one, you'll love it. As I researched this book, the ham makers profiled continually loaded me up with samples of their products, so I was forced to get creative in using them. This is a breakfast dish I made one morning while trying to clear the fridge of some inventory from those trips and that summer's canning season.

INGREDIENTS

2 eggs
1 teaspoon water
1 ounce spinach leaves, medium dice
1 ounce cooked country ham, small dice
½ ounce pickled jalapeño slices, small dice

PROCEDURE

After breaking eggs into a mixing bowl, add about 1 teaspoon of water and scramble eggs. The water renders the eggs fluffier via steam and agitation. Heat a nonstick pan on high until hot. Coat pan with spray oil, add spinach and country ham and sauté 1 minute or less. Add eggs and let set 15 to 20 seconds; sprinkle diced jalapeños around the mixture. With pan still on high heat, use a heatproof rubber spatula to gently scramble eggs, allowing uncooked eggs to flow into spaces made by scrambled eggs. Move quickly to avoid browning. Remove cooked eggs to warmed plate and serve.

Note: Since the peppers and ham already are salty, I recommend you don't salt the dish at all, or at least until you've had a bite or two.

Smokin' Good Bloody Mary

INGREDIENTS (IN A SHAKER WITH ICE)
1 1/2 ounces Finlandia Vodka (omit for an alcohol-free version)
6 ounces tomato juice
1/4 ounce liquid smoke
1/2 teaspoon horseradish
dash of Worcestershire sauce
squeeze of lime

ADDITIONAL INGREDIENTS
cayenne pepper
celery salt
1 slice country ham

PROCEDURE
Shake and strain into tall glass with ice rimmed with cayenne and celery salt. Garnish with a slice of country ham, folded accordion-style on a skewer.

To make rimmed glass, rub a lime wedge around lip of glass and dip into a mixture of celery salt and cayenne pepper on a plate. Note that you can adjust the pepper to taste.

John Varanese's Sweet Potato Biscuits

John Varanese's sweet potato biscuits fall into the "crack appetizer" category. When the chef-owner of Varanese Restaurant in Louisville, Kentucky, served these at the James Beard House in New York City, they were devoured. They're perfect not only with country ham but also with smoked turkey.

INGREDIENTS

4 cups all-purpose flour
1 cup brown sugar
3 tablespoons baking powder
1 tablespoon baking soda
1 tablespoon ground cinnamon
1 tablespoon salt
½ pound butter, cold and cut into small cubes
4 cups roasted sweet potatoes, baked and mashed
spray oil

PROCEDURE

Preheat oven to 400 degrees Fahrenheit. Combine flour, brown sugar, baking powder, baking soda, cinnamon and salt. Cut butter into flour until crumbly. Add sweet potatoes and mix completely, but avoid overmixing. Using rolling pin or hands, carefully flatten dough to ¾-inch thickness and cut biscuits, preferably with a metal ring cutter, although a Collins glass will work. (At this stage, biscuits can be frozen for later use. Just thaw and bake as normal.) Lightly spray baking pan and place biscuits on pan. Bake 8 minutes or until lightly browned. Cool, slice, add a smear of apple butter to one side and follow with paper-thin slices of your favorite country ham.

Granny Cardin's Country Ham and Red-eye Gravy with Angel Biscuits

Sondra Powell, owner of Red Hot Roasters Coffee in Louisville, provided this recipe from her grandmother, Pauline Cardin. Her recipe calls for shortening, but Pauline told her granddaughter, "You can use lard in place of shortening in anything. People just started using shortening to make things lighter." Amen, Granny! Note that the following biscuit recipe is made one day and then used the next, so plan accordingly.

Fried Country Ham and Red-eye Gravy

INGREDIENTS
2 teaspoons lard or bacon fat (or 1 tablespoon fat trimmed from ham)
6 slices country ham ¼-inch thick
½ cup freshly brewed black coffee

PROCEDURE
On medium-high heat, render ham fat for cooking or just add lard or bacon fat. In skillet, brown ham, remove to a separate dish and keep warm. Reduce skillet heat to medium, but do not let heat to smoking. Scrape brown bits loose from skillet and add coffee to skillet. Bring to a boil then lower to simmer, allowing flavors to mingle. Taste the red-eye gravy. If too bitter, add a 1 tablespoon of water to adjust flavor. Pauline recommends that you "keep it rich but not too much coffee to overpower the ham flavor." Correctly done, the mixture should look like fisheyes in the skillet. Return ham to the skillet, cover, place in oven and bake at 350 degrees Fahrenheit 30 to 45 minutes. Serve over hot angel biscuits (following) with ham on the side.

Angel Biscuits

INGREDIENTS
1 pack dry yeast
2 tablespoons warm water (100 degrees Fahrenheit)
2 cups buttermilk
3 tablespoons sugar
1 teaspoon salt
2 cups all-purpose flour
1 teaspoon baking soda
1 tablespoon baking powder
¾ cup shortening or lard
spray oil

PROCEDURE

Dissolve yeast in water, allow 5 minutes to bloom and then combine with buttermilk, sugar and salt in mixing bowl. Combine flour, baking soda and baking powder together in a separate bowl and cut in shortening or lard. Add liquid ingredients to dry and mix lightly, but do *not* knead. Refrigerate overnight. Preheat oven to 450 degrees Fahrenheit the next day, pinch off desired amount, knead, roll out and cut. Lightly spray baking pan, transfer biscuits to pan and go directly to the oven without allowing biscuits to rise. Bake biscuits 10 minutes, let cool slightly, slice and add open-faced to plates. Place warm ham and red-eye gravy over top.

Belinda's Buttermilk Biscuits

With these arguably perfect biscuits, Belinda Holland won the country ham biscuit contest at the 2013 Trigg County Country Ham Festival. As a judge for the contest, I can vouch that these are excellent. Holland stressed two keys to perfect biscuits: cold ingredients work best, so chill all ingredients at least 2 hours before using; also, chill the mixing bowl as called for in the directions.

INGREDIENTS

2 cups self-rising flour (she prefers White Lilly), chilled overnight in the refrigerator
6 tablespoons unsalted butter, cold and cubed
¾–1 cup whole cultured buttermilk (not low-fat)

PROCEDURE

Preheat oven to 450 degrees Fahrenheit. In a food processor bowl fitted with standard blade, combine flour and cubed butter. Pulse six to eight times until mixture is coarse like cornmeal. Remove mixture from processor bowl and place in a chilled mixing bowl. With a wooden spoon, make a well in the center of the flour-butter mixture. Add ¾ cup buttermilk into well and mix with spoon, just until combined. Mixture should be tacky. If dry, add remaining buttermilk.

On a cold, floured surface, such as marble or granite, turn out flour-buttermilk mixture. Gently pat out dough to a ½-inch thickness. Using hands, fold dough over five times, pressing lightly. With hands, gently press out dough to form 1-inch-thick disc. Using a floured biscuit cutter, cut out eight to ten biscuits.

Lightly grease a baking sheet using the wax paper cover from the butter stick. Move biscuits to pan and place them ½ inch apart. (Holland bakes hers on a well-seasoned cast-iron griddle.) Bake 10 to 12 minutes on middle shelf until biscuits rise. To brown biscuit tops, switch oven to broiler and broil 1 to 2 minutes, watching the entire time.

Allan Benton's Red-eye Gravy

Although chefs around the country would never think of heating Benton's Smoky Mountain Country Ham, if Allan Benton says it's best cooked with red-eye gravy, who's going to argue with him?

INGREDIENTS
2 slices country ham, about ¼-inch thick
1 teaspoon vegetable oil, as needed
½ cup fresh, hot coffee, divided in two
1 tablespoon brown sugar, firmly packed
hot biscuits

PROCEDURE
Trim fat from ham slices and place fat only in large cast-iron skillet; set ham aside. Cook fat over medium heat until rendered, about 3 minutes. If there is too little fat rendered as a result, add oil. Pour ¼ cup coffee into skillet, add brown sugar and stir until melted. Place ham slices in skillet and cover. Cook mixture until steaming lightly, remove lid and reduce just until ham browns. Transfer ham to plate and keep warm. Remove fat pieces from pan and add remaining coffee. Raise to medium-high and cook, stirring to remove any bits from pan bottom, about 2 minutes. Serve hot with ham and biscuits.

From Clifty Farms Country Meats

The following are two recipes from Clifty Farm's website. For several more tasty options, visit www.cliftyfarm.com/recipes.html.

Hot Country Ham Dip

INGREDIENTS
8 ounces cream cheese, softened
1 cup sour cream
½–1 cup Clifty Farm Boneless Cooked Country Ham, chopped
¼ cup onion, finely minced
½ teaspoon garlic powder
1 tablespoon butter
1 cup pecans, chopped
½ teaspoon Worcestershire sauce

PROCEDURE
Preheat oven to 350 degrees Fahrenheit. Combine cream cheese, sour cream, country ham, onion and garlic powder in small bowl and place in baking dish. Melt butter and sauté pecans. Add Worcestershire and sprinkle mixture over baking dish. Refrigerate until serving time. Bake for 20 minutes. Serve hot with crackers or raw vegetables. Also good served cold.

Cracklin' Cornbread

INGREDIENTS
2 cup self-rising cornmeal
1¼ cups buttermilk
1 egg, beaten
2 ounces Clifty Farm cracklins (can be purchased online at www.cliftyfarm.com)

PROCEDURE
Preheat oven to 450 degrees Fahrenheit. Generously grease round layer cake pan and heat in oven. Measure cornmeal into bowl and gradually add buttermilk; add beaten egg and cracklins. Pour into hot pan and bake for 10 to 15 minutes.

Country Ham Quiche

INGREDIENTS
3 eggs
$\frac{1}{2}$ cup Bisquick
$\frac{1}{2}$ cup butter or margarine, melted
$1\frac{1}{2}$ cup milk
$\frac{1}{4}$ teaspoon salt
dash of pepper
1 cup grated Swiss cheese
$\frac{1}{2}$ cup Clifty Farm Ham, finely chopped
4 ounces mushrooms, sliced

PROCEDURE
Preheat oven to 350 degrees Fahrenheit. Place eggs, Bisquick, butter, milk, salt and pepper in blender in small amounts and blend. When all ingredients are in, blend briefly once more to ensure uniformity. Pour mixture into greased 9-inch deep-dish pie pan. Sprinkle in cheese, Clifty Farm Country Ham and mushrooms and press into custard mixture with back of tablespoon. Bake at 350 degrees Fahrenheit for 45 minutes, remove and allow to cool 10 minutes before cutting and serving.

Ryan Rogers's Country Ham Ice Cream

So, country ham isn't for dessert? Try telling that to Ryan Rogers, chef-owner of Feast BBQ in New Albany, Indiana. The classically trained chef turned high-tech barbecuer loves experimenting with foods, and here's an excellent example of his creativity. Please note that this procedure requires that the country ham be soaked for two days in half-and-half, as well as an additional 24 hours of chilling, before making the mix into ice cream. Budget your time accordingly.

INGREDIENTS
1 pound country ham trimmings, diced small (often these are packaged and available at grocery stores, or you can buy whole ham slices, remove all edge fat and then dice the meat)

3 cups half-and-half
1 cup sugar, divided
5 egg yolks

Procedure

Soak ham in half-and-half for 24 to 48 hours (Rogers prefers 48). Heat a pot of water to simmering. In a mixing bowl that will fit snugly atop the water pot, combine ½ cup sugar with egg yolks and beat until combined; over simmering water, cook mixture until it becomes pale yellow, whisking gently but constantly. Avoid working any air into the mixture.

Add the remaining ½ cup of sugar to the half-and-half and country ham mixture and heat to 180 degrees Fahrenheit (scalding but not boiling). Add slowly to egg yolk and sugar mixture while whisking thoroughly to incorporate. Let chill, preferably for 24 hours, then strain through a *chinois* or other fine-mesh strainer. Add to ice cream machine to churn until firm. Remove from churn to a sturdy freezer container and freeze at least 4 hours. Serve with any sweet biscuit.

Dallas McGarity's Country Ham and Ricotta Ravioli with Bourbon-Mustard-Mushroom Cream and Kale

No spoiler alert here. The title alone hints that this is a dish for the fully initiated cook, which, not by accident, describes the cooking of Dallas McGarity, executive chef and partner at Marketplace Restaurant in Louisville, Kentucky.

Ingredients for Ravioli Filling

1 cup country ham, finely minced
3 cups ricotta cheese
1 tablespoon garlic, finely minced
1 tablespoon Italian flat-leaf parsley, finely minced
1 cup Parmesan cheese, grated
salt and pepper to taste

Procedure

Mix all ingredients together with hands until evenly incorporated.

Ingredients for Pasta Dough
1 teaspoon salt
4 cups semolina flour
1 cup warm water
1 egg plus 2 teaspoons milk for egg wash

Procedure
In a large bowl, combine salt and flour. Add and work in water slowly until proper texture is achieved—neither too tough nor too soft. (This requires practice to learn, but once you get it, you know it.) Wrap dough in plastic wrap and rest 20 minutes. Beat eggs and milk and set aside.

To make ravioli, roll out dough into sheets and use a circle cutter to cut into round shapes at least 2½ inches across; larger ravioli are fine, too. Place spoonful of ravioli filling onto one circle and brush edge with egg wash. Place another round of pasta on top and, using the tips of a fork, press to close.

Ingredients for Garnish
olive oil for sautéing
1 tablespoon finely minced garlic
2 cups kale, neatly chopped (I prefer Lacinato, but Tuscan, dinosaur or black work as well)
salt and pepper to taste

Procedure
In a sauté pan over high heat, add oil and garlic, sautéing briefly, followed by kale. Cook until wilted. Season with salt and pepper, set aside and keep warm.

Ingredients for Bourbon-Mustard-Mushroom Cream
1 tablespoon olive oil
2 cups mushrooms, cleaned and chopped roughly (any you like; I prefer cremini)
1 tablespoon garlic, finely chopped
1 tablespoon rosemary, finely chopped
3 ounces quality bourbon
1 quart heavy cream
2 tablespoons whole grain mustard
1 tablespoon butter
salt and pepper to taste

PROCEDURE

In large sauté pan, heat olive oil over medium-high heat; sauté mushrooms, garlic and rosemary until mushrooms are well done. Meanwhile, boil water for ravioli. Remove pan from the heat, add bourbon, return to heat and bring mixture to a simmer. Add ravioli to water and cook until al dente. Drain and remove to a single bowl or individual plates. Add heavy cream and reduce until it coats the back of a spoon lightly. To finish, add mustard and butter and pour over poached ravioli to serve.

Traditional Baked Country Ham (from Finchville Farms Country Hams)

INGREDIENTS

1 whole Finchville Farms Country Ham
$\frac{1}{2}$ cup vinegar
2–3 dozen cloves
1 cup brown sugar

PROCEDURE

Place ham in large roasting pan skin side up. Cover two-thirds of ham with water, add vinegar to water and place cover on roaster. Move ham and roaster onto stove, bring liquid to a boil and then lower heat to a simmer. Simmer 15 minutes per pound or until a meat thermometer inserted into the thickest part of the ham reads 160 degrees Fahrenheit. Remove ham from water and cool. Remove skin and excess fat. If desired, debone.

Preheat oven to 350 degrees Fahrenheit. Move ham to shallow roasting pan. Score fat in diamond pattern and stud with cloves. Pat brown sugar onto ham and bake 30 minutes. Remove from oven, cool to room temperature and slice thinly. To store remaining ham after cooking, wrap well in plastic film and refrigerate to prevent drying. Cured country ham will remain safe in the refrigerator for one month.

Oven-Roasted Country Ham, Bag Method (from Rice's Country Hams)

PROCEDURE

Remove hock. Soak ham overnight in water in a large container, such as a sanitized five-gallon plastic bucket (available at most hardware stores). Preheat oven to 350 degrees Fahrenheit. Remove ham and wash thoroughly with warm water, using a bristle brush. Place ham in a large oven roasting bag suitable for turkeys. To bag, add as much water as possible while still leaving room to secure the tie on the bag without leaking. Place ham and bag with water in bottom part of broiling pan, skin side up.

Move to oven, reduce heat to 225 degrees Fahrenheit and bake for 30 minutes per pound. Remove ham from oven and drain water from bag. Remove exterior fat and skin and internal bones. Serve warm or, if you prefer, wrap tightly in aluminum foil and cool in refrigerator. When cold, slice ham thinly or take to a butcher for thin slicing by machine.

Boiled Country Ham

The Rice family credits longtime customer Peggy McKnight with this recipe.

INGREDIENTS
3 liters Coca-Cola (not diet)
2 liters ginger ale (not diet)
1½ cinnamon sticks
1½ cups white sugar
¾ cup vinegar
4 bay leaves
1 teaspoon whole cloves
1 whole country ham

PROCEDURE

Soak ham in water overnight. Wash ham thoroughly with warm water, using a bristle brush. Place all ingredients except ham into a large pot and mix. Add ham, bring mixture to a boil, reduce to a simmer and cover pot. Cook 2½ hours and then turn off heat. Let cool, covered, overnight. Remove ham from mixture and discard mixture. Skin ham and place on serving platter.

INGREDIENTS FOR HAM GLAZE
1½ cups brown sugar
12 cloves, whole

PROCEDURE
In a heavy-bottomed saucepot, combine brown sugar and cloves and heat slowly until mixture liquefies. Pour or brush over the ham. Slice ham and serve.

Country Ham Quiche (from Harper's Country Hams)

INGREDIENTS
½ pound cooked country ham, diced
½ pound Swiss cheese, sliced
2 unbaked pie shells
4 eggs
1 tablespoon flour
2 cups half-and-half
½ teaspoon cayenne pepper
½ teaspoon nutmeg
1 tablespoon butter, melted

PROCEDURE
Alternate layers of ham and cheese in pie dishes. Beat eggs; add flour, half-and-half, spices and butter. Pour egg mixture over cheese and ham. Bake at 375 degrees Fahrenheit for 50 to 60 minutes and serve.

Country Ham Spread

Ingredients
1 pound cooked country ham, ground
3 eggs, boiled, shelled and mashed
1½ cups Miracle Whip or mayonnaise
1½ cups sweet pickle relish

Procedure
Mix ingredients and chill. Serve on bread or crackers of your choice.

Cheesy Country Ham Potatoes

Ingredients
1 package frozen hash browns
½ pound fully cooked country ham, diced
1½ sticks margarine
1 pound Velveeta, cubed
1 pint half-and-half

Procedure
Place potatoes in 9x13-inch greased pan. Top with other ingredients. Bake at 350 degrees Fahrenheit for 30 minutes and serve.

Country Breakfast Casserole

Ingredients
1 package Harper's country ham pieces
6 to 8 slices bread (torn into pieces)
½ cup grated cheese (your choice)
2 cups milk
6 to 8 eggs, beaten
salt and pepper to taste

PROCEDURE

Cook ham by stir-frying in skillet on medium heat for 1 to 2 minutes per side. In large baking dish, layer torn bread, ham and cheese. Add milk to beaten eggs and season with salt and pepper. Pour egg mixture over meat, cheese and bread. Refrigerate overnight. Bake at 350 degrees Fahrenheit for 35 minutes prior to serving.

Country Ham Rolls

INGREDIENTS

2 packages prebaked dinner rolls (in foil pan)
$\frac{1}{2}$ pound sliced country ham, fully cooked
2 6-ounce packages mozzarella cheese (sliced)

INGREDIENTS FOR BASTING

$\frac{1}{2}$ cup margarine, melted
$\frac{1}{2}$ tablespoon poppy seeds
$1\frac{1}{2}$ teaspoons Worcestershire sauce
1 teaspoon onion powder

PROCEDURE

Do not separate rolls. Slice tops from rolls in one piece. Place bottoms in baking pan. Layer ham and cheese onto bottom layer of rolls and replace top. Combine basting ingredients, mix well and brush tops of rolls. Bake covered with foil at 350 degrees Fahrenheit for 30 minutes or until cheese is melted. Serve hot.

Hamloaf Hors d'Oeuvre

INGREDIENTS

2 8-ounce packages cream cheese
1 bunch green onions, chopped
1 7-ounce package fully cooked
    country ham

dash liquid smoke
dash Worcestershire sauce
dash garlic powder
dash hot sauce

PROCEDURE

Blend all ingredients until fully incorporated. Serve on bread or crackers.

Ham Hocks 'n' Cabbage Dinner

INGREDIENTS
2 quarts water
3 ham hocks

ADDITIONAL INGREDIENTS
2 heads cabbage, quartered
6 potatoes, peeled

PROCEDURE
Place water and ham hocks in pot, bring to boil and then reduce heat to simmer. Cook about 2 hours; remove hocks and wrap in foil to keep warm. Place additional ingredients into pot with ham broth and cook 20 minutes more. Once cooked, place cabbage and potatoes on serving platter; slice meat from hocks and serve with the vegetables.

Baked Whole Ham (from The Hamery)

INGREDIENT
1 whole country ham

PROCEDURE
Trim off about ⅛ inch of lean, fat and skin from the face and sides of ham, or until fresh meat is exposed. Using a kitchen saw or a hacksaw with a new and sanitized blade, cut off about 2 inches of the hock and 1 inch of the butt and cut off the aitch bone. Soak ham in cool water for 2 to 3 hours. Place ham in an oven cooking bag with one quart of water. Tie bag securely so the water will rise half way up the ham. Do not puncture bag. Place ham on a rack in a shallow, uncovered pan with the fat side up so the ham will baste itself. Roast for 30 minutes per pound of ham at 200 degrees Fahrenheit; to be precise, use a meat thermometer and cook until the internal temperature reaches 155 degrees Fahrenheit. Glaze if desired and cool before slicing.

Cheddar and Ham Cheese Ball

INGREDIENTS
24 ounces of cream cheese, softened
1 bunch green onions, chopped
1 medium bell pepper, diced finely
1 cup cooked country ham, ground
3 teaspoons Worcestershire sauce
16 ounces cheddar cheese, grated

PROCEDURE
Mix cream cheese, onions, bell pepper, ham and Worcestershire sauce thoroughly. Blend cheese into mixture and taste for seasoning. Refrigerate 1 hour and then remove and form mixture into a ball. Cover with plastic and refrigerate at least 30 minutes more. When ready to serve, remove 10 minutes beforehand and place on serving dish.

Ground Country Ham Salad

INGREDIENTS
½ pound ground country ham, cooked
½ tablespoon sugar
½ tablespoon spicy brown yellow mustard
⅓ cup mayonnaise
¼ jar India Relish
¼ cup onion, chopped
¼ cup celery, chopped
3 eggs, boiled, peeled, cooled and chopped

PROCEDURE
Mix all ingredients together. Spread on a fresh biscuit and enjoy.

The Hamery's Angel Biscuits

Ingredients
1 cup buttermilk
¼ teaspoon baking soda
2 teaspoons sugar
2 teaspoons yeast
1 cup warm water (about 105 degrees Fahrenheit)
4 cups all-purpose flour
¾ cup shortening

Procedure
Mix together buttermilk and baking soda. Mix sugar, yeast and 1 cup of warm water in a 16-ounce glass. Mix flour and ¾ cup of shortening, such as butter-flavored Crisco, until crumbly. When yeast-sugar mixture rises out of the top of glass, add to flour and shortening, followed by buttermilk and soda. Mix all until smooth, cover with plastic wrap and let stand until it doubles in size.

Roll out on floured cutting board. Flour the top; flatten and fold each end to the middle to make a ball. Flip over so the smooth side is up and roll out and cut ⅜-inch-thick biscuits. Let rise again and cook at 325 degrees Fahrenheit until slightly brown.

Volare's Vitello Saltimbocca with a Kentucky Taste

In this recipe from the Volare Italian Ristorante (Louisville, Kentucky), executive chef Joshua Moore leans on country ham's similarities to prosciutto ham from Italy.

Ingredients
salt and pepper to taste
12 2-ounce slices of veal strip loin, pounded with a meat mallet under a
    sheet of heavy plastic
flour for dredging veal and thickening sauce
¼ cup extra virgin olive oil
2 teaspoons of fresh sage, chopped

8 ounces white wine
8 ounces chicken stock
12 paper-thin slices of country ham
4 ounces mozzarella cheese, shredded
4 ounces butter, cubed

Procedure

Preheat oven to 400 degrees Fahrenheit. Salt and pepper each side of each piece of veal, dredge in flour and set aside. In a sauté pan over medium-high heat, add extra-virgin olive oil. Once shimmering, sauté veal until light golden brown. Add chopped sage and deglaze pan with white wine. Add chicken stock and remove veal.

On a sheet pan, cover veal with country ham slices and mozzarella. Place in the oven and cook until golden brown. Reduce wine and stock by one fourth. Quickly dredge butter in flour and add to wine and stock. Move veal from oven to plates and pour sauce over top.

INDEX

ABOUT THE AUTHOR

S teve Coomes is a freelance food, spirits and
travel writer. After working more than a
decade in restaurants as a server and a chef,
he began writing about the business in 1991.
He served sixteen years as editor of multiple
restaurant industry publications before setting
out on his own in 2007. He is a regular
contributor to several restaurant and consumer
magazines, a restaurant blogger, a radio show
and podcast host and a ghostwriter for multiple
clients. He lives in Goshen, Kentucky, with his
wife and son.

Photo by Nancy LaRocca.